THE GOLDEN AGE COOKBOOK

THE

Golden Age

COOKBOOK

BY PHYLLIS MacDONALD

DRAWINGS BY MARGOT TOMES

Doubleday & Company, Inc.
Garden City, New York
1961

To Georgene

Library of Congress Catalog Card Number 61–11296
Copyright © 1961 by Phyllis MacDonald
All Rights Reserved
Printed in the United States of America
First Edition

CONTENTS

THE GOLDEN AGE COOKBOOK

*A book to help older folks lead happy, healthy lives;
for those also who are interested in
the well-being of their parents or older friends.*

Chapter One

PLANNED HEALTH AND

HAPPINESS

If we seriously accept the fact that at any age level, tasty, adequate foods, well prepared and regularly eaten, will help prolong vigor and the enjoyment of retirement years, we are paying ourselves an extra health dividend. Those people over sixty-five in good health are sure to owe some of their vitality to past food habits. Whether they have consciously eaten the right foods or not, they probably have. Those who feel a bit run-down most of the time would do well to recognize that there is no substitute for a visit to the doctor. He will be the first to say that there is no retirement from good, regularly eaten meals.

Whether one is in a low- or high-income group, it is important to include adequate milk, milk products, green and yellow vegetables, citrus fruits and tomatoes in the meals day after day. They all have their own particular work to do in keeping us well. Every day, no matter what age, we all need protein foods for the upkeep of body tissues and bones. Starches and sugars as well as some fats are required for energy and warmth. Although your doctor may prescribe vitamins in capsule form, don't discount foods as valuable sources. Citrus fruits and tomatoes, the richest sources of vitamin C, supply not only that important vitamin, but also valuable bulk, minerals, and enjoyable flavor. Vitamin-capsule supplements should be considered as supplements and not substitutes for the natural vitamins in well-prepared, tasty foods. We need less food, of course, as we grow older and our activities are less, but we continue to need all of the right kinds of foods as long as we live.

Since this is primarily a cookbook and not a nutrition text, the menus and recipes given on the following pages are not individually analyzed for food values, but they do meet the needs of normal, well men and women of retirement age. Let them be used as patterns for further meal planning. Those with dietary problems may find them a guide, too, but only with their doctors' endorsement. The menus planned here are simple and are neither exhausting nor expensive to prepare. Though planned for a family of two with a modest income, they are tasty enough to suit any palate. If the budget allows, more expensive cuts of meat or fresh fruits out of season rather than applesauce or stewed apricots, etc., may be preferred.

Though pension checks may be low, the tea-and-toast, coffee-and-cake snack habit is not the answer. This bad habit curtails the appetite for the milk, vegetables, and meats we need daily and will not pay dividends of prolonged vitality. Too frequent nibbling may add unneeded pounds without giving needed nutrition. Meals for one, if living alone, or for two, if both are enjoying retirement together, should be high spots of each day. They can be prepared and eaten with re-laxed enjoyment. No bowl of soup or peanut butter sandwich, tasty though they may be, deserves to be called a meal if it is eaten in the dull setting of a corner drainboard.

This does not mean that you need a hard-to-iron linen tablecloth every meal in order to set an attractive table. Let a simple paper or plastic place mat and paper napkin play its part in making your table charming—and in conserving your energy. Cheerful and inexpensive, these come in a variety of patterns, so change your table scenery often.

To help you plan the right meals with assurance, these very few do's and don't's are given to act as check-list reminders:

• Have at least one hot food at every meal.

• Include two servings a day of lean meat *or* poultry *or* fish *or* cheese *or* eggs.

• Be sure you have one serving of a citrus fruit or vegetable daily.

• Serve either a whole-grain cereal or enriched bread every meal, too.

• A dark green or deep yellow vegetable for vitamin A at least once a day.

• Daily, too, a serving of potato *or* rice *or* macaroni *or* spaghetti for energy's sake and for downright good eating.

• Plan several days' menus at a time for economy in buying—economy, too, in preparation.

• Seldom serve fried foods, rich gravies, or heavy pastries. If you do make a pie, and of course you will sometimes, serve a roast or simple casserole dish that meal, not fried meat, *and* gravy, *and* pie.

• Eat at regular times. Let every meal contribute to your enjoyment of that day.

Chapter Two

THE RIGHT KITCHEN
FOR YOU

It is probably true to say that all homemakers, whether twenty or seventy, waste some energy needlessly. Good though organization and equipment may be, it is never absolutely perfect. In our later years planning for a minimum of bodily wear and tear is more important than ever.

Whether you live, when retired, in the home you have owned for years, are planning a new home for the two of you, or live in a room or small apartment in your children's home, a kitchen can be planned to meet your needs. Organization or reorganization will save many a backache, prevent accidents, allow your more limited energy to be used for recreation and hobbies. Count the times you reach overhead or stand on a stool to pull a casserole from a high shelf. Keep looking for these weak spots that can be changed to make meal preparation more convenient.

If you are building a new home, such things as a wall oven, eye-level cupboard shelves, garbage disposal and dishwashing units (budget permitting) all help in conserving energy. If you are moving into a room in your children's home and long for occasional privacy, make yourself a tiny pushcart or counter-top kitchen, using small electrical appliances. With no more cooking facilities than an electric hot plate, tasty meals can be yours. An all-in-one hot main dish, prepared on the burner, a salad, bread, and made-ahead dessert are all you need. Coffee or tea can be in the making while this one-hot-plate dinner is being served.

Other small appliances can be added from time to time until your counter-top kitchen, though requiring almost no space, is as adequate as two people could wish. With a table oven, a fry pan, an electric saucepan, coffee maker, and toaster, you are in business to serve meals as usual. An electric can opener (drop a hint for one at Christmas time) makes opening cans of all sizes a push-button procedure. Newer automatic appliances are of stainless steel instead of heavy, hard-to-lift aluminum, and can, for the most part, be completely immersed in water. The newer electric fry pans and Dutch ovens have another plus: two lug-type handles, opposite each other, make lifting them easier, carrying them safer. If you are rebuilding a kitchen or replacing equipment, there is much to be said for a small-appliance workshop. Each unit does its own job. Used independently, or two or three at a time, these appliances do the work of a large, harder-to-clean range. For safety's sake such kitchens are worthy of serious consideration. They have no gas flame to blow out in a draft, no pilot light to go off.

For safety's sake, too, no one can take chances with improperly stored foods. Adequate refrigeration in all homes, no matter what the size of the kitchen, is a must. A freezing compartment has its advantages. With it, shopping trips can be less frequent and meal planning more varied. However, if yours is a studio home, tiny plug-in refrigerators closely resembling TV cabinets come in a variety of wood finishes. Appearing to be walnut or mahogany furniture, they properly refrigerate enough foods for a day or two and make housekeeping in a room possible when no other refrigerator is conveniently near.

Insurance companies tell us that cuts, burns, and falls right in our own homes are high on the list of crippling accidents. Such accidents need not spoil the enjoyment of your retirement years. Let a well-installed knife rack prevent the cuts that often result from reaching into a drawer for a knife.

Limit utensil and equipment space to easily reached areas. It makes sense. Let climbing up on a stool or ladder be a thing of the past from this minute on. Saucepans and mixing bowls that are light enough to lift with ease makes sense, too. Big bowls aren't needed often when cooking for a twosome. Why cling to heavy cast-iron pots? More than one toe has been broken by dropping one. A good hard tumble is no fun either. Spilled grease or water are often the cause of one. So wipe up the minute something is spilled and avoid such accidents.

Chapter Three

MEALS TO ENJOY AND
WISE USE OF
PLANNED LEFTOVERS

Though preparing meals for two, or for one, if living alone, is far less work than preparing for a hungry family, there are new habits to acquire if the day-by-day menus are to be varied and interesting. Dabs of leftover morsels that are bound to accumulate even with the best of twosome planning can make or break a retirement budget, depending upon what becomes of them. The four weeks' menus which follow and the recipes given will help establish a "planning ahead pattern" that results in tasty, easy-to-prepare meals, planned not only for enjoyment, but for continued good health. Half a cup of cooked green beans added to a salad, one third of a cup of tuna stirred into an omelet, bits of this and that added to macaroni and cheese—this is the magic that makes cooking for two fun.

Let breakfast be one requiring little cooking, but breakfast there must be. By lunchtime, unless energy foods are eaten at that important first meal of the day, the body is really working at a disadvantage. Dinner in the middle of the day rather than at night may be a wise habit to adopt now. Dinner need not be a complicated affair, exhausting to prepare. Let it be built around a one-dish meal and a simple dessert. Then with a light supper there is more time and energy left to enjoy a leisurely, cozy evening, perhaps more opportunity for a restful sleep to follow naturally.

If you prefer to continue a lifelong dinner-at-night habit, and the thought of your main meal at noon makes you unhappy, *of course* eat dinner at night. Try though to avoid rich foods at that last meal of the day, especially if you tend to toss and turn.

When our supper menus call for foods prepared in advance at a noon dinner, use the supper menu for luncheon the following day.

As to that word "optional" following tea or coffee in the menus which follow, it is up to you and your doctor whether you serve them often, seldom, or never. This, of course, applies not only to those over sixty-five, but to everyone. Not really foods, since they in themselves give us no nourishment, these flavorful, soothing beverages are extras, not essentials.

There are recipes for all dishes starred (*). These follow the planned menus. These recipes can also be located by consulting the Index.

Summer

MENUS AND RECIPES

Whether the weather is impossibly hot or just right from a temperature standpoint, three well-planned meals are just as important in the summer as other times of the year. Piecing from the refrigerator won't do if health and vigor are to continue. At least one hot food a meal is a good rule to follow. That doesn't need to make you a summertime hot-kitchen martyr. Now is the time to give your oven a bit of a vacation, at least on the hottest days, and to enjoy main dishes and desserts prepared with a minimum of effort from top-of-the-range favorites.

MENUS

SUNDAY

BREAKFAST

Glass of Orange Juice
Ready-to-Eat Cereal
Buttered Cinnamon Toast
Crisp Bacon (optional)
Coffee
Glass of Milk

DINNER

*Stewed Chicken with Noodles
Buttered Summer Squash or Fresh or Frozen Wax Beans
Heated Packaged Rolls   Butter or Margarine
Shredded Lettuce   *Cottage Cheese Dressing
*Five Minute Crumb Crust Ice Cream Pie
Tea

SUPPER

Cup of Chicken Consommé
*Cream Cheese and Dried Beef Sandwich
Sliced Tomatoes
More Ice Cream Pie from Dinner or Packaged Cookies
Tea
Glass of Milk

MONDAY

BREAKFAST

Canned Grapefruit and Orange Segments
Heated Packaged Muffins   Butter   Jelly
Scrambled Eggs
Coffee
Glass of Milk

DINNER

*Braised Beef Roll-Ups with Steamed Green Onions
Instant Whipped Potatoes
Stewed Tomatoes
*Jellied Lime and Vegetable Salad
Bread   Butter
Fresh Peaches with Cream and Sugar
Packaged Cookies
Tea

SUPPER OR LUNCHEON

*Split Pea Soup with Deviled Ham
Crackers
Stewed Fresh Plums
*Toasted Pound Cake Slices with Cinnamon Sugar
Glass of Milk

TUESDAY

BREAKFAST

Fresh Berries and Cream or Apricot Juice (canned)
Ready-to-Eat Cereal
Soft Cooked Egg
Buttered Toast
Coffee
Glass of Milk

DINNER

*Double Boiler Spaghetti Scallop
Buttered Peas
Pickled Beets
*Pear Halves Royal
Frosted Graham Crackers
Glass of Milk
Tea (optional)

SUPPER

Hot Vegetable Juice Cocktail (V-8)
*Crunchy Tuna and Vegetable Salad
Thin Bread and Butter Sandwiches
*Lemon-Rice and Apricot Pudding
Glass of Milk

WEDNESDAY

BREAKFAST

Stewed Prunes with Orange Juice
Quick-Cooking Cereal
Buttered Toast   Jam
Coffee
Glass of Milk

DINNER

*Pan-Broiled Chicken Livers with Mushrooms
Parsley Buttered New Potatoes
Buttered Green Beans (fresh or canned or frozen)
Vanilla Pudding with *Spiced Cherry Sauce
Tea

SUPPER

Cup of Cream of Tomato Soup
Chilled Spaghetti Scallop with Catsup
Crisp Lettuce Sandwiches
Stewed Fresh or Dried Fruit
Packaged Cookies
Glass of Milk
Tea

THURSDAY

BREAKFAST

Stewed Fresh Figs or Apricots or Frozen Grapefruit Juice
Ready-to-Eat Cereal
Packaged Frozen Pancakes or Waffles   Syrup
Coffee
Glass of Milk

DINNER

Chilled Consommé with Lemon Slice
*Surprise Tomato Meat Balls with Steamed Rice
Buttered New Carrots
Rolls   Butter or Margarine
*Mint and Applesauce Sundae
Packaged Oatmeal Cookies
Tea or Coffee

SUPPER

Chilled Apple Juice
*Western Sandwich for Two
*Marinated Long Green Beans
Small Wedge of Watermelon or
Sliced Fresh Peaches and Cream
Glass of Milk

FRIDAY

BREAKFAST

Glass of Orange Juice
Ready-to-Eat Cereal
Packaged Corn Muffins   Butter   Jelly
Coffee
Glass of Milk

DINNER

*Crab Newburg on Toast
Buttered Baby Lima Beans
Celery Hearts Stuffed with Chive Cream Cheese
*Individual Strawberry Shortcakes
Glass of Milk
Tea

SUPPER

*Clam and Vegetable Soup
Crackers
Cold Canned Salmon with Mayonnaise
Lemon Sherbet
Packaged Cookies
Half Glass of Milk

SATURDAY

BREAKFAST

Grapefruit Sections (frozen or canned)
*Hot Shredded Wheat with Poached Egg
Buttered Toast
Coffee
Glass of Milk

DINNER

*Top Stove Chicken Fricassee with Gravy
Mashed Canned Sweet Potatoes or Instant Whipped Potatoes
Tomato Salad   *Harlequin Dressing
Stewed Fresh Cherries or Canned Bing Cherries
Packaged Cookies
Glass of Milk
Tea

SUPPER

*Black Bean Rabbit on Corn Muffins
Fruit Salad with Cottage or Cream Cheese
*Unbaked Bread Pudding
Glass of Milk
Tea

Stewed Chicken and Noodles

In just two or three minutes of your own time, the timer set then as a reminder, this recipe goes to work to finish itself.

> *2 chicken legs or 1 double breast, split*
> *1 cup boiling water*
> *½ teaspoon paprika*
> *½ teaspoon salt*
> *Dash pepper*
> *½ teaspoon onion flakes*
> *2 cups packaged noodles*
> *½ cup canned chicken gravy*
> *½ teaspoon parsley flakes (optional)*

Choose the chicken parts you prefer. Wash and dry them well. Pour the boiling water into a 3-quart saucepan with a tight-fitting cover, or into a Dutch oven. Add the chicken parts, paprika, salt, pepper, and onion flakes. Cover and simmer for about ½ hour or until chicken is fork-tender. Pour the noodles over the chicken, cover again and continue to cook for about 10 minutes or until noodles are done. Stir in the canned chicken gravy and the parsley flakes. Makes 2 servings.

Cottage Cheese Dressing

¼ cup cottage cheese
¼ cup bottled French dressing
2 pimiento-stuffed olives, chopped

Blend the ingredients in a small jar and chill until used. Makes about ⅓ cup or enough for two salads. Use within 3 days.

Five Minute Crumb Crust Ice Cream Pie

Before church or early in the morning make this "special" dessert. Ten minutes does it from start to finish. You'll say it is too good not to serve often, too easy to call work.

¾ cup packaged cereal crumbs
    or graham cracker crumbs
3 tablespoons melted butter or margarine
1 tablespoon sugar
½ cup milk
1 package instant chocolate pudding mix
1 pint vanilla ice cream, slightly softened

Before church, combine the crumbs, butter or margarine, and sugar, stirring with a fork to blend well. Press the crumb mixture into an 8-inch pie pan, bringing crumbs well up to the rim. Chill crumb crust while preparing the filling.

Pour the milk and pudding mix into a bowl. Beat with an egg beater for 1 minute. Then spoon in the ice cream and beat the mixture smooth. Pour the filling into the crumb crust and chill until dinnertime. Makes 1 8-inch pie—enough for dinner and supper with a bedtime dividend.

Filling for Cream Cheese and Dried Beef Sandwiches

Whether you use sandwich buns or slices of bread, this recipe makes enough for two hearty main-dish supper sandwiches.

> *¼ cup snipped dried beef*
> *1 3-ounce package cream cheese*
> *½ teaspoon prepared mustard*
> *Lettuce*

Snip the beef into bits with a kitchen scissors. Blend together the beef, cheese, and mustard, adding a teaspoon or so of milk, if necessary, to make the mixture easy to spread. Use half of the filling for each sandwich. Top filling with crisp lettuce. Makes 2.

Braised Beef Roll-Ups with Steamed Green Onions

> *½ pound round steak, cut ¼-inch thick*
> *½ teaspoon salt*
> *1 teaspoon minced onion*
> *Dash pepper*
> *1 tablespoon chili sauce*
> *1 tablespoon shortening*
> *½ cup water*
> *4 to 6 small green onions, tops and all*
> *½ cup canned beef gravy*

Have the butcher slice the beef so that it is the right thickness. Then at home, about an hour before dinner, cut the meat into

4 pieces as near the same size as possible. Combine the salt, pepper, onion, and chili sauce. Spread this mixture thinly over the beef and roll each piece up securely, jelly-roll fashion. Fasten the rolls with a small skewer or toothpick. Melt the shortening in a skillet with a cover (an electric fry pan if you have one) and brown the beef rolls lightly on all sides. Pour the water into the pan. Cover and simmer for 30 minutes. Then add the green onions and a bit more water, if necessary, to keep liquid simmering around the beef. Cover the pan again and continue to cook for 10 more minutes or until the onions are tender. Just before serving stir in the gravy and bring it to a boil. Makes 2 servings of 2 roll-ups each.

Jellied Lime and Vegetable Salad

> ½ cup boiling water
> ¼ cup plus 1 teaspoon (half a package)
>   lime-flavored gelatin dessert
> ¼ cup grated raw carrot
> 1 teaspoon parsley flakes
> ¼ teaspoon instant onion
> ¼ cup cold water or buttermilk
> ½ cup cottage cheese
> Crisp lettuce

Right after breakfast, before the day warms up, pour the boiling water over the lime gelatin and stir until the gelatin is dissolved. Blend in the remaining ingredients. Pour mixture into 2 custard cups and chill until firm. Before dinner unmold the salads onto crisp lettuce. Makes 2 servings.

Split Pea Soup with Deviled Ham

Tasty and filling without being too filling.

> 1 10½-ounce can split pea soup
> 1 cup milk
> 1 2¼-ounce can deviled ham or 2 slices packaged boiled
>   ham (diced) plus ⅛ teaspoon dry mustard

Combine all ingredients in a saucepan and heat over medium heat until steaming hot. Stir to blend. Makes 2 hearty supper main-dish servings.

Toasted Pound Cake Slices with Cinnamon Sugar

> 1 individually packaged slice pound cake
> 1 teaspoon butter or margarine
> ⅛ teaspoon cinnamon
> 1 teaspoon sugar or 1 teaspoon prepared cinnamon sugar

Toast pound cake in the electric toaster. Butter it and sprinkle with the combined cinnamon and sugar. Cut in half and serve warm. Makes 2 servings.

Double Boiler Spaghetti Scallop

Though we have used ham in this recipe, it is equally good if diced cooked chicken luncheon meat, canned tuna, or crab are used in place of the ham.

1 cup uncooked spaghetti, broken into 1-inch lengths
⅔ cup grated American cheese
½ teaspoon instant onion
1 10½-ounce can mushroom soup
½ cup diced ready-to-eat ham
½ teaspoon salt
Dash pepper
2 tablespoons milk

Cook spaghetti in 1 quart of boiling water until tender—about 12 minutes. Drain. Combine spaghetti and remaining ingredients in the top of a double boiler. Cover and set boiler top in place over boiling water. Heat for 20 minutes or until cheese is melted and the mixture steaming hot. Fill 2 custard cups with the mixture and chill them for a supper main dish another night (see Wednesday). The remaining hot spaghetti makes 2 generous main-dish dinner servings.

Pear Halves Royal

2 medium-sized fresh pears
1 cup boiling water
¼ cup sugar
Dash salt
¼ cup grape jelly

Peel, halve, and core the pears. Combine boiling water, sugar, and salt in a saucepan. Bring to a boil and add pear halves. Cover and simmer for 10 minutes or until pears are tender. Stir in the jelly. Remove from heat and serve warm or chilled. Makes 2 servings. If you prefer, use 4 canned pear halves. Combine ½ cup juice drained from the canned pears and the ¼ cup of grape jelly. Heat juice and jelly slowly, stirring until well blended. Pour it over the pear halves and serve warm or chilled.

Crunchy Tuna and Vegetable Salad

1 3½-ounce can tuna
½ cup cooked mixed vegetables
1 hard-cooked egg, diced
1 small green onion
Dash salt
¼ cup crushed cheese crackers
⅓ cup mayonnaise
Crisp lettuce leaves

Flake tuna with a fork. In a small bowl combine tuna, vegetables, and egg. Slice in green onion, tops and all. Add salt, cracker crumbs, and mayonnaise. Toss lightly with a fork to blend. Chill and serve on crisp lettuce. Makes 2 servings.

Lemon-Rice and Apricot Pudding

Not too tart, not too sweet. This recipe makes two large cereal-bowl servings for a lighter-than-usual supper, or four average-sized dessert servings for a heavier meal.

1 package lemon pudding mix (not instant)
½ cup sugar
1¼ cups canned apricot juice
1 egg
¾ cup water
½ cup cooked rice
2 to 3 whole fresh or canned apricots, split in half

Combine pudding mix, sugar, ¼ cup of the apricot juice in a saucepan. Beat the egg well and stir it into the mixture in the pan, blending well. Add the rest of the apricot juice and the water. Cook over medium heat, stirring constantly, until thick and bubbling. Stir in the rice and pour the pudding into dessert dishes. Chill. Serve topped with apricot halves, with or without light cream, as desired.

Pan-Broiled Chicken Livers with Mushrooms

> *1 tablespoon butter or margarine*
> *1 teaspoon minced onion*
> *½ pound chicken livers*
> *¼ teaspoon salt*
> *Dash pepper*
> *1 3- or 4-ounce can sliced mushrooms*

Heat butter in a small skillet. Add onion, chicken livers, salt, and pepper. Cook slowly until liver is browned on all sides. Add mushrooms, juice and all. Continue to cook, stirring occasionally, until liquid from mushrooms is absorbed and liver is done—about 10 minutes. Makes 2 servings.

Spiced Cherry Sauce

> *⅓ cup cherry preserves*
> *1 tablespoon water*
> *1 to 2 whole cloves*

Blend all ingredients in a small saucepan. Bring to a boil;

cool. Remove cloves and chill. Serve over instant vanilla pudding made from package mix. Makes sauce for 2 servings.

Surprise Tomato Meat Balls with Steamed Rice

½ slice bread
⅓ pound (5 to 6 ounces) lean ground beef
¼ teaspoon salt
Dash pepper
1 12-ounce can V-8 juice

Tear bread into crumbs. Combine crumbs, beef, salt, and pepper. Blend well. Form into balls the size of a walnut (about 8). Bring juice to a boil in a saucepan. Drop in meat balls and simmer, uncovered, for 12 to 15 minutes or until sauce is bubbly thick. Serve meat balls and sauce over steaming hot rice. Makes 2 servings.

Mint and Applesauce Sundae

2 tablespoons mint jelly
⅓ cup canned applesauce
Vanilla ice cream

Combine jelly and applesauce in a custard cup or small jar. Place it in a saucepan and pour hot water around the cup almost to the top. Heat slowly until jelly melts. Then beat smooth with a fork and chill. Makes ½ cup sundae sauce for vanilla ice cream.

Western Sandwich for Two

2 strips bacon
3 eggs
2 tablespoons milk
¼ teaspoon salt
Dash pepper
½ teaspoon instant onions or 1 teaspoon minced onion
1 tablespoon chopped green pepper (optional)

Cook bacon in a medium-sized skillet until crisp. Drain it on a paper towel. Beat the eggs in a bowl and crumble in the bacon. Stir in the remaining ingredients. Pour the egg mixture into the bacon drippings in the pan and cook slowly for 1 to 2 minutes or until the eggs are beginning to "set." Then with a spatula mold them into two rounds. Turn to brown both sides. Serve in split, buttered sandwich buns or between buttered bread slices. Makes 2 servings.

Marinated Long Green Beans

1 cup cooked or canned long green beans
⅓ cup bottled French dressing
½ teaspoon dill seeds or a sprig of fresh dill (optional)
¼ teaspoon celery salt

Drain beans and arrange them in a shallow pan. Combine remaining ingredients and pour over the beans. Chill. Makes 2 tangy servings.

Crab Newburg on Toast

An elegant main dish from pantry-shelf items. Just the one to serve when it's too hot to want to shop.

> *1 7½-ounce can crab meat (undrained)*
> *2 tablespoons flour*
> *1 teaspoon instant onion*
> *¼ teaspoon salt*
> *Dash mace (optional)*
> *½ teaspoon grated lemon rind (optional)*
> *½ cup evaporated milk and ½ cup water*
> *Buttered toast*

Empty the crab into a small bowl and remove the spiny pieces. Then for an absolutely "can't lump" sauce combine flour, onion, salt, mace, lemon rind, milk, and water in a saucepan. Beat with a fork until blended (about half a minute). Add butter. Cook slowly, stirring, until the mixture is smooth and thickened. Stir in the crab and heat 1 minute. Serve on buttered toast. Makes 2 to 3 servings.

Individual Strawberry Shortcakes

Packaged sponge cake layers, available in most groceries today, make it possible to serve shortcakes and dozens of other easy-to-prepare desserts without a bit of baking. Wrapped in foil or other moisture-proof paper, the unused portion keeps for days, all ready to use when needed.

> *2 tablespoons sugar*
> *1 cup washed, sliced fresh strawberries*
> *1 packaged sponge layer (about 6½ inches diameter)*
> *Cream or whipped cream (optional)*

Sprinkle the sugar over the berries and chill until dessert time. Then with a 2-inch biscuit cutter, cut 2 rounds from the sponge layer. Split the rounds in half crosswise. Fill and top each with berries. Serve with cream or whipped cream, if desired. Makes 2 servings. There will be plenty of cake bits left to make Saturday's Unbaked Bread Pudding.*

Clam and Vegetable Soup

> 3 tablespoons (about ½ package)
>   dry tomato-vegetable soup mix
> 1½ cups water
> 1 7½-ounce can minced clams (undrained)

Pour the whole package of soup mix into a bowl. Stir it to blend thoroughly. Measure the 3 tablespoons of mix into a saucepan. Return the rest of the unused mix to its original package and seal the edges. Save for soup another day.

Add the water to the mix in the pan, cover, and boil for 10 minutes. Pour in clams; heat to boiling. Makes 2 servings.

Hot Shredded Wheat with Poached Egg

> ½ cup hot milk
> 2 shredded wheat biscuits
> 2 poached eggs

Pour hot milk over the shredded wheat and let it "steep" for 1 minute. Make a depression in the top of each biscuit with the back of a spoon. Slip a poached egg into the depressions in the biscuits and serve at once. Makes 2 servings.

Top Stove Chicken Fricassee with Gravy

2 chicken legs or 1 double breast, split
1 tablespoon flour
¼ teaspoon salt
Dash pepper
⅛ teaspoon powdered thyme (optional)
2 tablespoons shortening or bacon drippings
½ cup water
½ cup canned chicken gravy

Wash chicken and dry it well. In a brown paper bag combine the flour, salt, pepper, and thyme. Shake the chicken pieces to coat them well in the flour mixture. Heat the shortening in a skillet with a tight-fitting cover, or in a Dutch oven. Brown chicken slowly, turning to brown on all sides. Add the water, cover, and simmer for 15 to 20 minutes or until chicken is tender. Pour in gravy, bring to a boil, and serve. Makes 2 servings.

Harlequin Dressing

A good way to use up chilled, cooked leftover vegetables to advantage.

⅓ to ½ cup chilled cooked vegetables
2 tablespoons mayonnaise
2 to 3 tablespoons French dressing

Blend all ingredients and serve over sliced tomatoes or shredded lettuce. Makes about ½ cup dressing.

Black Bean Rabbit on Corn Muffins

¾ cup canned condensed black bean soup
½ cup grated American cheese
2 tablespoons catsup
2 packaged corn muffins

Measure the soup into a saucepan. Pour the rest of the soup into a refrigerator dish; cover and store in the refrigerator for another meal. To the soup in the saucepan add the cheese and catsup. Heat very slowly, stirring constantly, until steaming hot. Toast and butter muffins. Serve rabbit over muffins. Makes 2 servings.

Unbaked Bread Pudding

1 cup sponge-cake cubes (cut from packaged cake layer)
½ package instant vanilla pudding mix (¼ cup of the
*   mix)*
1¼ cups milk

Divide sponge cake cubes into 2 custard cups. Pour the pudding mix and the milk into a bowl and beat for 1 minute. Then pour it over the cake cubes in the cups. Chill. Serve with Spiced Cherry Sauce*, or just "as is." Makes 2 servings.

Autumn

MENUS AND RECIPES

One morning you wake up and sniff the air. Someone is burning a pile of raked-up leaves. A cozy season, autumn! Nature's harvest of juicy grapes, mellow squash, and garden-ripened tomatoes is on hand to give meals tempting variety.

Let well-planned meals supply energy to carry you, in good health, through the winter months ahead.

MENUS

SUNDAY

BREAKFAST

Melon in Season or Stewed Nectarines
Poached Egg on Toast
Bacon (optional)
Glass of Milk
Coffee or Tea

DINNER

*Baked Parmesan Veal Chops
Baked Potatoes
*Old-Fashioned Succotash in Cream
Green Salad   *Dill French Dressing
Bread   Butter or Margarine
*Apple-Raisin Pie for Two
Half Glass of Milk
Tea (optional)

SUPPER

*Quick New England Clam Chowder   Crackers
Tomato and Cottage Cheese Salad
*Banana Coconut Crisps
Tea or Coffee (optional)

MONDAY

BREAKFAST

Orange Juice
Quick-Cooking Cereal
Coffee Cake
Glass of Milk or Hot Chocolate
Coffee or Tea (optional)

DINNER

Pan-Broiled Liver with Crisp Bacon
*Hashed Browned Potato Pancake for Two
*Braised Yellow Squash and Tomatoes
Bread   Butter or Margarine
*Plum Duff
Glass of Milk
Coffee or Tea (optional)

SUPPER

Cream of Vegetable Soup
*Baked Stuffed Tomatoes with Ham
Rolls   Butter or Margarine
Fruit Salad
Packaged Oatmeal Cookies
Half Glass of Milk
Tea or Coffee (optional)

TUESDAY

BREAKFAST

Sliced Bananas with Cream
Ready-to-Eat Cereal (optional)
Scrambled Eggs
Toast
Glass of Milk
Coffee or Tea

DINNER

Baked Sausage Patties
*Stuffed Acorn Squash
Sliced Tomato Salad   French Dressing
Packaged Refrigerator Biscuits
Butter or Margarine   Honey
Stewed Fresh Figs or Canned Figs with Cream
Chocolate Icebox Wafers
Half Glass of Milk
Tea or Coffee (optional)

SUPPER

Small Glass of Tomato Juice
*Mealy Baked Potatoes with Cheese and
Chives   Crisp Bacon
Shredded Lettuce   Thousand Island Dressing
Bread   Butter or Margarine
*Crunchy Coconut Grahams
Hot Chocolate or Glass of Milk

WEDNESDAY

Half Grapefruit
Quick-Cooking Cereal
Cinnamon Rolls   Butter or Margarine
Glass of Milk
Coffee or Tea

*Baked Noodle Casserole de Luxe
Buttered Green Beans
Celery Sticks
Bread   Butter or Margarine
*Cranberry and Apple Betty
Half Glass of Milk
Tea or Coffee (optional)

*Scrambled Eggs and Vegetables on Corn Muffins
*Creamy Rice Pudding with Cherry Sauce
Half Glass of Milk
Tea (optional)

THURSDAY

BREAKFAST

Grapefruit Juice
Packaged Frozen Waffles or Pancakes   Syrup
Crisp Bacon
Glass of Milk
Coffee or Tea

DINNER

Small Glass of Apple Cider
*Escalloped Ham and Hubbard Squash
Stewed Fresh Tomatoes
Bread   Butter or Margarine
*Baked Fresh Pears
Glass of Milk
Tea or Coffee (optional)

SUPPER

Chicken Consommé with Rice   Crackers
Pineapple and Cream Cheese Salad
Small Peanut Butter Sandwiches
Chocolate Pudding
Half Glass of Milk
Tea or Coffee (optional)

FRIDAY

BREAKFAST

Stewed Apricots
Poached Eggs on Toasted Buttered Muffins
Glass of Milk
Coffee or Tea

DINNER

*Poached Salmon with Parsley Butter   Steamed Rice
Buttered Chopped Spinach
Lettuce and Tomato Salad
Bread   Butter or Margarine
*Lemon Meringue Pie for Two
Half Glass of Milk
Tea or Coffee (optional)

SUPPER

*Tuna Salad Burgers on Sandwich Buns
Broiled Tomato Slices
Fruit Jello with *Lemon Sauce
Glass of Milk
Tea (optional)

SATURDAY

BREAKFAST

Canned Grapefruit and Orange Segments
Quick-Cooking Cereal
Toast   Marmalade
Glass of Milk
Coffee or Tea

DINNER

*Stewed Chicken with Country Style Butter-Browned Noodles
Buttered Yellow Squash or Carrots
Green Salad   Thousand Island Dressing
Bread   Butter or Margarine
Packaged Gingersnaps
Half Glass of Milk
Tea or Coffee (optional)

SUPPER

Hot Clam Juice or Tomato Juice
Crackers
*Eggs Benedict
Fresh Grapes or Stewed Fresh Plums
Glass of Milk
Tea or Coffee (optional)

RECIPES

Baked Parmesan Veal Chops

Before church or early in the morning, fix chops, all ready to bake. Bake them before dinner in the same oven with the Apple-Raisin Pie.*

> 2 shoulder veal chops (about 1 pound)
> ½ teaspoon salt
> Dash pepper
> 1 tablespoon shortening
> 1 8-ounce can tomato sauce
> 2 tablespoons grated Parmesan cheese
> 1 teaspoon parsley flakes

Wash chops and dry them well on a paper towel. Combine flour, salt, and pepper in a pie pan. Coat chops well on both sides in flour mixture. Heat fat in a skillet and brown chops slowly in hot fat, about 10 minutes on each side. Arrange them in a 1-quart baking dish with a cover. Pour tomato sauce over. Sprinkle with the cheese and parsley flakes. This much do before church or ahead of time, if you wish. Then, 45 minutes before dinner, heat the oven to 400°F. (moderately hot). Bake chops, covered, for 25 minutes. Uncover and continue to bake for 10 to 15 minutes, or until very tender. Makes 2 servings. One pound may sound like a lot of chops for two, but don't forget—shoulder chops have that big bone.

Old-Fashioned Succotash in Cream

> *1 ear corn*
> *½ to ¾ pound fresh lima beans, shelled*
> *   (⅔ cup shelled limas)*
> *1 teaspoon butter or margarine*
> *1 teaspoon minced onion*
> *¼ teaspoon salt*
> *Dash pepper*
> *¼ cup light cream or half milk-half cream*

Cook corn in boiling salted water. Cool. Cut kernels from the ear. Meanwhile, cook the lima beans in boiling, salted water for about 20 to 25 minutes or until just tender. Drain. Heat the butter in a small saucepan. Add onion and cook 1 minute. Stir the corn, limas, salt, pepper, and cream into onion. Heat. Makes 2 servings.

Or, instead of fresh vegetables, use ½ cup canned whole-kernel corn and ½ cup cooked, drained frozen lima beans.

Dill French Dressing

Early in the day, at least several hours before dinner, pour ¼ cup of your favorite brand of bottled French dressing into a custard cup. Stir in ¼ teaspoon of dill seeds, or snip a small sprig of fresh dill into the dressing. Let it stand. See what a tangy difference the dill makes!

Apple-Raisin Pie for Two

Prepare this pie, ready to bake, before church. Then, while dinner cooks, in a matter of 40 minutes or so, the pie will be done, too. Serve it warm, with or without cream.

½ package (1 cup) piecrust mix or 1 stick mix
¼ cup seedless raisins
1½ cups thinly sliced cooking apples (2 small apples)
¼ teaspoon grated lemon rind
1 teaspoon flour
¼ cup brown sugar, packed
¼ teaspoon ground cinnamon
Dash salt

Prepare piecrust as package directs. Divide it into two small balls. Measure raisins into a mixing bowl. Peel and slice apples into the bowl. Add lemon rind, flour, brown sugar, cinnamon, and salt. Toss with a fork to coat fruit well. Roll out half of the dough on a floured board or pastry cloth and fit it into a 5-inch aluminum or Pyrex pie pan. Pour fruit mixture into this bottom crust. (It will be piled high, but it will fit in.) Roll out the rest of the dough for the top crust. Prick it toward the center with a fork, making vents through which steam can escape. Fit top crust over apples. Trim crust ½ inch larger than the rim of the pan. Flute dough around the edge.

After church, heat oven to 400°F. (moderately hot oven). Bake pie for 40 minutes, or until nicely browned and steaming hot.

Quick New England Clam Chowder

1 tablespoon butter or margarine
2 slices bacon, cut in strips
2 tablespoons minced onion
1 cup boiling water
1 small potato, pared and diced
½ teaspoon salt
Dash pepper
1½ cups milk
2 tablespoons light cream
1 10-ounce can minced clams

Melt butter in a saucepan. Brown bacon in it for 1 to 2 minutes. Add onion; sauté 1 to 2 minutes. Add boiling water, potato, salt, and pepper. Cook, covered, until potatoes are tender (about 10 minutes). Add milk, cream, and clams. Heat. Makes 2 generous main-dish portions.

Banana Coconut Crisps

2 bananas
1 tablespoon light cream
¼ cup packaged cornflake crumbs or cornflakes,
rolled fine
1 teaspoon sugar
¼ teaspoon cinnamon
2 tablespoons butter or margarine
1 teaspoon lemon juice
1 tablespoon shredded coconut

Peel bananas and cut in 1-inch chunks. Dip in cream. Blend cornflake crumbs, sugar, and cinnamon. Roll banana chunks in this mixture. Melt butter in a small skillet; then sauté bananas until tender, turning to brown all sides (2 to 3 minutes). Sprinkle with lemon juice. Serve sprinkled with coconut. Makes 2 servings.

Hashed Browned Potato Pancake

2 medium-sized potatoes, well scrubbed
1 teaspoon minced onion
¼ teaspoon salt
⅛ teaspoon pepper
2 tablespoons bacon drippings
1 tablespoon butter or margarine

Early in the day, if you like, cook potatoes in their jackets until they are tender. Drain and cool them. Half an hour before dinnertime, skin potatoes. Grate them into a bowl, using a medium to coarse grater. Add onion, salt, and pepper. Toss with a fork to blend.

In a medium-sized skillet heat the bacon drippings and butter over low heat. Pour potatoes into the skillet and pack them firmly with a spatula. Then, with your spatula, pull potatoes away from the edges of the pan, making a small "trough" around them. Cook over low heat for 12 to 15 minutes, or until jets of steam rise up through the surface. Using a spatula, fold potato pancake in half. Roll it out onto a heated serving dish. Makes 2 yummy servings.

Braised Yellow Squash and Tomatoes

> 1 small yellow summer squash (about ¾ pound)
> 1 medium-sized, red-ripe tomato
> 1 small onion
> 1 tablespoon butter or bacon drippings
> 2 tablespoons water
> Salt
> Pepper

Wash squash. Dice it in 1-inch cubes. Pour boiling water over the tomato and let it stand 1 minute. Peel tomato and onion. Slice both. Heat butter or drippings and water in a saucepan. Add squash and onion. Sprinkle with salt and pepper. Cover and cook over low heat for 8 to 10 minutes, or until squash is almost tender. Add tomato. Cover again, and cook for 4 to 5 minutes or until tomato is done. Makes 2 servings.

Plum Duff

> 4 fresh plums (about ½ pound)
> 2 tablespoons sugar
> Dash grated nutmeg
> ⅓ cup biscuit mix
> 2 teaspoons sugar
> 2 teaspoons melted butter or margarine
> 2 tablespoons milk
> ½ teaspoon sugar, blended with a dash of ground cinnamon

Heat the oven to 350°F. (moderate). Cut plums in half; remove pits and slice into two custard cups. Sprinkle 1 tablespoon of the sugar over plums in each cup. Sprinkle with nutmeg. In a small bowl combine the biscuit mix, 2 tea-spoons sugar, melted butter, and milk. Stir to blend well. Spoon batter over plums. Then sprinkle with cinnamon sugar. Bake in preheated oven for 30 minutes or until bubbling hot and lightly browned. Makes 2 servings.

Baked Stuffed Tomatoes with Ham

> *2 firm tomatoes*
> *Dash salt*
> *1 slice packaged boiled ham, diced*
> *¼ cup crumbled saltine-type crackers*
> *1 teaspoon minced onion*
> *1 tablespoon melted butter or margarine*

Heat oven to 375°F. (moderately hot). Scoop out the centers of the tomatoes. Sprinkle the cavities with salt. Dice the scooped-out pulp and combine it with the remaining ingredients. Fill tomatoes with the stuffing, mounding it high on each. Bake in preheated oven for 20 to 25 minutes or until tomatoes are fork-tender. Makes 2.

Stuffed Acorn Squash

> *1 large acorn squash (about 1½ pounds)*
> *2 strips bacon*
> *1 tablespoon sugar*
> *1 peeled, finely diced cooking apple*
> *⅔ cup crumbled saltine-type cracker crumbs*
> *1 teaspoon grated onion*
> *1 tablespoon bacon drippings*
> *¼ teaspoon salt*

Heat oven to 375°F. (moderately hot). Wash squash and split it in half. Scoop out the seeds. Bake, cut side down in the pan, for 30 minutes. Meanwhile, fry bacon until crisp. Drain on a paper towel and crumble it into bits. Combine bacon and remaining ingredients. When the timer rings at the end of 30 minutes, turn squash. Stuff with apple mixture and bake for another 30 minutes or until done. Makes 2 servings.

If serving sausage patties, as suggested, with this squash, arrange them in a pie pan and bake along with squash for about 45 minutes.

Mealy Baked Potatoes with Cheese and Chives

2 baking potatoes
Dash salt
¼ cup sharp-cheese spread
1 teaspoon minced chives
Paprika

Select uniform baking potatoes. Scrub them with a brush. Rub the skins with shortening or salad oil. Heat oven to 400°F. (moderately hot). Bake potatoes for 50 to 60 minutes. To test for doneness, squeeze them gently, using a pot holder to protect your hands. If soft, they are done. Remove them from the oven. Cut a deep crisscross in the top of each. Press, using pot holders, to fluff them open. Sprinkle each with salt. Top with cheese and chives. Return to the oven for 2 minutes, until cheese melts. Serve topped with a dash of paprika. Makes 2 servings.

Crunchy Coconut Grahams

6 square graham crackers or 3 double crackers
3 to 4 tablespoons shredded coconut
1 tablespoon brown sugar
Dash salt
1 tablespoon soft butter or margarine

Just before supper arrange crackers on a baking sheet. Combine coconut, brown sugar, salt, and butter. Blend with a fork. Spread coconut mixture over crackers and bake in preheated oven (same 400°F. oven as supper main dish) for 10 minutes or until crispy brown. Or, if you prefer, broil them 5 inches from heat for 2 to 3 minutes.

Baked Noodle Casserole de Luxe

2 cups uncooked packaged noodles
1 slice bread
⅓ cup grated packaged American cheese
1 cup milk or ½ cup
    evaporated milk and ½ cup water
2 slightly beaten eggs
½ teaspoon salt
⅛ teaspoon dry tarragon leaves (optional)

Cook noodles in boiling, salted water. Rinse and drain. Tear bread into crumbs. Alternate layers of noodles, crumbs, and grated cheese in a greased 1-quart casserole. Combine milk, eggs, salt, and tarragon. Pour over noodles. Heat oven to 375°F. (moderately hot). Set pan of noodles into a larger pan. Pour in hot water to within 1 inch of the top of the noodle casserole. Bake in preheated oven for 40 to 45 minutes or until lightly browned. Makes 2 generous servings.

Cranberry and Apple Betty

> 2 tablespoons butter or margarine
> 1 cup soft bread crumbs (2 slices bread)
> 2 medium-sized cooking apples
> ½ cup raw cranberries
> ¼ cup sugar
> ⅛ teaspoon cinnamon
> Dash salt

Heat oven to 375°F. (moderately hot). Melt butter in a small saucepan. Tear bread into crumbs and stir into the butter, coating crumbs well. Peel apples and slice them thin. Combine apples, cranberries, sugar, cinnamon, and salt. Add the buttered crumbs, and pour into a 1-quart baking dish. Cover and bake in preheated oven for 30 minutes. Uncover and continue to bake for 15 to 20 minutes or until lightly browned. Makes 2 servings.

Scrambled Eggs and Vegetables on Corn Muffins

> 3 eggs
> 2 tablespoons milk
> ½ cup drained canned mixed vegetables
>   or ½ cup leftover vegetables
> ¼ teaspoon Worcestershire sauce (optional)
> ¼ teaspoon salt
> 2 teaspoons butter or margarine
> 2 toasted packaged corn muffins

Beat eggs well. Stir in milk, drained vegetables, Worcestershire sauce, and salt. Heat butter or margarine in a small skillet. Pour egg mixture into skillet. Stir over low heat until as firm as you like. Serve over toasted corn muffins. Makes 2 servings.

Creamy Rice Pudding with Cherry Sauce

This creamy treat comes from Scandinavia. There, at Christmas time, even Julltomten, the invisible little gnome who lives in each home, gets his dish. To the delight of the children, he sneaks out in the night and licks his dish clean. The family cat, of course, is the one who benefits.

> 1 cup milk
> 1 teaspoon unflavored gelatin
> 2 tablespoons raw rice
> 2 tablespoons sugar
> Dash salt
> 2 tablespoons chopped blanched almonds
> 1 whole almond
> ½ teaspoon vanilla extract
> ½ cup heavy cream, whipped
> ¼ cup cherry preserves
> 1 tablespoon water

Scald ¾ of the cup of milk in the top of a double boiler. Pour the remaining ¼ cup of milk into a cup. Sprinkle the gelatin over it and let stand. When tiny bubbles appear around the edge of the hot milk, stir in the softened gelatin, rice, sugar, and salt. Cover and cook over simmering water for 45 minutes, or until rice is soft and mealy. Stir in the chopped almonds, vanilla, and the whole almond. Cool to room temperature. Fold in whipped cream and chill. Makes 2 generous servings.

Why a whole almond? Tradition has it that the lucky one who gets it will have the best of luck for months to come.

For Cherry Sauce, blend the preserves and water. Serve over the pudding.

Escalloped Ham and Hubbard Squash

1 pound Hubbard squash
⅓- to ½-pound slice ready-to-eat ham
2 tablespoons brown sugar
Dash salt
¼ cup pineapple or orange juice
1 tablespoon butter or margarine

Scrape seeds and stringy portion from squash. Then, to make it easy to peel (and this sometimes is a hard job), place squash in a colander or strainer over boiling water. Cover and steam it until nearly tender—about 30 minutes. Cool. Heat oven to 375°F. (moderately hot). Cut ham in two pieces. Arrange them in a greased 1-quart casserole. Cover ham with thin slices of squash. Sprinkle with brown sugar and salt. Pour juice over. Dot with the butter or margarine. Bake, uncovered for 45 minutes, or until squash is mealy. Makes 2 servings.

Baked Fresh Pears

2 firm, ripe pears
¼ cup sugar
½ cup water
1 tablespoon sugar
3 tablespoons orange juice
Sprinkling of ground cinnamon

Wash, core, and peel pears. Stand them up in a small baking dish. Heat the oven to 375°F. (moderately hot). In a small saucepan combine the ¼ cup of sugar and the water. Bring to a boil and boil for 1 minute. Pour over the pears. Cover and bake for 40 to 50 minutes or until tender. Uncover. Sprinkle with the 1 tablespoon of sugar. Drizzle with the orange juice and bake for another 10 minutes. Serve warm or chilled, sprinkled with cinnamon. Makes 2.

Poached Salmon with Parsley Butter

> *1 salmon steak cut ¾ inch thick*
> > *(about ¾ pound)*
>
> *¼ cup milk*
> *¼ cup water*
> *2 lemon slices*
> *¼ teaspoon salt*
> *1 teaspoon melted butter or margarine*
> *2 teaspoons parsley flakes*

Cut salmon into two pieces. Place it in a small skillet or saucepan. Add the milk, water, lemon slices, and salt. Cover and cook over low heat for 15 to 20 minutes or until salmon is fork-tender. Remove carefully to serving platter. Drizzle with butter or margarine. Sprinkle with parsley. Makes 2 servings.

Lemon Meringue Pie for Two

This pie, as you'll see, pays an added dividend. When your pie is finished and cooling, your sauce for supper's dessert is cooling too . . . both done at the same time.

> *½ cup piecrust mix*
> *1 tablespoon cold water*
> *1 package lemon pie filling (not instant)*
> *½ cup sugar*
> *2 eggs, separated*
> *1¾ cups water*
> *¼ cup sugar*

Combine piecrust mix and water, tossing with a fork to blend. Form dough into a ball. Roll it out on a floured board or cloth. Fit it into a 5-inch aluminum or Pyrex pie pan. Prick the entire surface of the crust with a fork. Heat oven to 425°F. (moderately hot). Bake crust 10 to 12 minutes or until lightly browned. Cool.

In a small saucepan, combine lemon filling mix, the ½ cup sugar, slightly beaten egg yolks, and water. Cook over medium heat, stirring constantly, until smooth, thick, and bubbling. Cool 5 minutes. Meanwhile, beat egg whites until soft and fluffy. Gradually beat in the ¼ cup sugar, beating until meringue is very stiff. Pour ½ cup of the lemon filling into a cup. Pour the rest of the filling into the pie shell. Spread about ¾ of the meringue over the lemon filling and return pie to the oven to brown meringue—about 5 minutes. Cool at room temperature. Makes 2 servings.

Lemon Sauce for Supper

Stir the ½ cup of lemon filling into the bit of leftover meringue. Chill. Thin with a little water and use as a sauce for fruit jello and other desserts.

Tuna Salad Burgers on Sandwich Buns

2 sandwich buns
1 teaspoon butter or margarine
1 3½-ounce can tuna
⅓ cup finely shredded lettuce
2 sliced stuffed olives
2 tablespoons mayonnaise

Split buns. Spread lightly with butter or margarine. Empty tuna into a bowl and add remaining ingredients, tossing lightly to blend. Serve buns filled with tuna mixture. Makes 2.

Stewed Chicken with Country Style Butter-Browned Noodles

If you had a Pennsylvania Dutch grandmother and ever ate her noodles, you may have wondered why yours never had quite that flavor. Prepare these and see if they don't. If you've *never* eaten butter-browned noodles, then you have a new treat in store.

> *2 chicken legs, or 1 double breast, split*
> *2 cups water*
> *½ teaspoon salt*
> *1½ cups packaged noodles*
> *1 tablespoon butter or margarine*
> *1 teaspoon flour*

Wash chicken and dry it on a paper towel. Combine chicken, water, and salt in a saucepan. Cover and cook over low heat until tender, about 35 to 40 minutes. Remove the chicken from the broth and keep it warm. Add more water, if necessary, to make about 1½ to 2 cups broth. Bring it to a boil; pour in noodles and cook 8 minutes or until noodles are tender. Drain noodles, saving the broth for soup. Meanwhile, in a small pan, heat the butter until frothy and lightly browned. Add the flour, stirring until mixture is a deep golden brown. Pour noodles into browned butter and toss them lightly with a fork to coat well. Makes 2 servings.

Eggs Benedict

1 split, toasted English muffin or 2 slices toast
Butter or margarine
2 slices packaged boiled ham
2 poached eggs
½ cup canned cream of celery soup
1 teaspoon lemon juice

Arrange one half of a buttered, toasted muffin on each serving plate. Top each with a slice of ham, then a poached egg. In a small saucepan heat together the soup and lemon juice. Pour soup over the eggs. Makes 2 servings.

Winter

MENUS AND RECIPES

Wintertime, of all seasons, gives the opportunity for leisurely mealtime enjoyment. Now is the time to feature baked casserole favorites and steaming hot bowls of cereal, and to enjoy an occasional baking spree. Now is the time to take especial notice that enough of the important foods—meats, vegetables, milk, and citrus fruits—are eaten. Those important foods do help in warding off colds and other wintertime ills.

SUNDAY

BREAKFAST

Stewed Dried Prunes and Apricots
Toasted English Muffins   Butter or Margarine
Poached Egg
Glass of Milk
Coffee

DINNER

*Baked Ham and Sweet Potato Casserole
Buttered Mixed Vegetables (canned or frozen)
Celery Sticks or Shredded Lettuce with Mayonnaise
Whole-Wheat Bread or Rolls
*Quick Apple Betty
Tea

SUPPER

Hearty Tomato Vegetable Soup
Crackers and Cheese
*Ambrosia
Glass of Milk
Tea (optional)

MONDAY

BREAKFAST

Sliced Bananas with Cinnamon Sugar and Milk
Poached Egg on Toast
Coffee or Tea
Half a Glass of Milk

DINNER

Small Glass of Grapefruit and Orange Juice
*Braised Lamb Shanks with Fluffy Rice
Bread or Rolls   Butter or Margarine
Tomato Salad   French Dressing with a
Few Dill Seeds Added
*Five Minute Peach Melba
Glass of Milk
Tea (optional)

SUPPER

Cream of Chicken Soup
Crackers
Cottage Cheese Salad with Grated Raw Carrot
*Crunchy Topped Gingerbread Square
with Applesauce
Half a Glass of Milk
Tea (optional)

TUESDAY

BREAKFAST

Orange Juice (frozen or canned)
Quick-Cooking Cereal
Corn Muffins
Jelly or Marmalade
Glass of Milk
Coffee

DINNER

*Meat Loaf for Two
Baked Potatoes
*Cream Chopped Spinach (fresh or frozen)
Bread or Packaged Biscuits   Butter or Margarine
*Gingerbread-Banana Shortcake
Glass of Milk
Coffee or Tea (optional)

SUPPER

Small Glass of Tomato Juice
*Scrambled Eggs with Chipped Beef and Mushrooms
Celery Sticks
Fruit Jello with *Quick Custard Sauce
*Homemade Graham Brownies or Packaged Cookies

WEDNESDAY

BREAKFAST

Orange and Grapefruit Segments (canned or frozen)
French Toast with Syrup or Preserves
Crisp Bacon (optional)
Glass of Milk
Coffee

DINNER

*Shepherd's Pie for Two (with vegetables)
Pineapple and Cottage Cheese Salad
Rolls or Bread   Butter or Margarine
*Refrigerator Pudding
Glass of Milk
Tea (optional)

SUPPER

*Broiled Meat Loaf, Tomato, and Cheese Sandwich
Shredded Lettuce   Thousand Island Dressing
Canned Peach Halves with Packaged Macaroons
Glass of Milk
Tea (optional)

THURSDAY

BREAKFAST

Sliced Bananas with Apricot Juice
Quick-Cooking Cereal
Packaged Heat-and-Serve Sausages
Whole-Wheat Toast   Butter or Margarine
Half Glass of Milk
Coffee

DINNER

*Swiss Steak for Two
Escalloped Potatoes (packaged)
Canned or Frozen Peas
*Tangy Carrot and Celery Slaw
Packaged Sponge Cups with Vanilla Ice Cream and
*Apricot Sauce
Half Glass of Milk
Tea (optional)

SUPPER

Steaming Hot V-8 Cocktail
*Deviled Ham French Toast with Apple Butter or Syrup
Pear and Cottage Cheese Salad
Packaged Cookies
Glass of Milk
Tea (optional)

FRIDAY

BREAKFAST

Blended Apricot and Orange Juice
Soft-Cooked Egg
Buttered Toast   Jelly or Cinnamon Sugar
Glass of Milk or Hot Chocolate
Coffee (optional)

DINNER

Hot Tomato Juice
*Escalloped Macaroni and Tuna
Buttered Wax Beans (frozen or canned)
Melba Toast
*Butterscotch Graham Cracker Pudding
Tea

SUPPER

*Shrimp and Corn Bisque
Shredded Lettuce Salad   Blended Catsup and French
Dressing
*Heavenly Hash or *Creamy Rice Custard
*Cinnamon Tea

SATURDAY

BREAKFAST

Temple Orange or Tangarines
Quick-Cooking Cereal with Brown Sugar and Hot Milk
Buttered Toasted Muffins   Jelly or Honey
Glass of Milk
Coffee

DINNER

*Baked Chicken with Fluffy Onion Rice
Buttered Asparagus (frozen or canned)
Tomato and Lettuce Salad   Pickle Relish Mayonnaise
Heated Packaged Rolls   Butter or Margarine
Compote of Mixed Stewed Dried Fruits
Half Glass of Milk
Tea

SUPPER

*Vegetable Omelet
Crackers
*Baked-Ahead Cheese-Glazed Apples
Glass of milk
Tea

Baked Ham and Sweet Potato Casserole

Here is the perfect Sunday midday dinner main dish. Easily prepared ahead of time, before church if you like, it is all ready to heat and serve in 30 minutes.

2 to 3 medium-sized sweet potatoes
1 slice ready-to-eat ham (about ½ pound)
¼ cup brown sugar, packed
¼ cup orange juice
⅛ teaspoon ground cinnamon
⅛ teaspoon salt
1 tablespoon butter or margarine

Ahead of time, cook unpeeled potatoes, cool, and remove skins. Grease a 1-quart baking dish. Cut ham in 2 pieces and place it in the bottom of the baking dish. Slice potatoes in half and arrange them over the ham. In a small saucepan, combine the brown sugar, orange juice, cinnamon, salt, and butter or margarine. Stir well and bring the mixture to a full, rolling boil. Pour it over the sweet potatoes and ham. The casserole may be covered and kept at room temperature for several hours. Thirty minutes before dinner heat the oven to 375°F. (moderately hot oven). Bake the ham and sweet potatoes covered, for 30 minutes, or until steaming hot. Makes 2 servings.

Quick Apple Betty

This Sunday dessert can be made ahead ready to bake after church in the same oven along with the Baked Ham and Sweet Potato Casserole.*

> *3 medium-sized cooking apples, peeled and thinly sliced*
> *⅓ cup brown sugar, packed*
> *⅛ teaspoon salt*
> *¼ teaspoon nutmeg*
> *¼ teaspoon cinnamon*
> *½ cup packaged graham cracker crumbs*
> *2 tablespoons melted butter or margarine*

Ahead of time, combine sliced apples, brown sugar, salt, and spices. Toss lightly with a fork to coat the apples well. Stir together the graham cracker crumbs and butter. Sprinkle half of the crumbs over the bottom of a greased 8-inch pie pan. Pour apple mixture over the crumb layer. Top with the remaining crumbs. Heat oven to 375°F. (moderately hot oven). Bake in preheated oven for 25 to 30 minutes or until apples are tender. Serve warm with light cream. Makes 2 servings.

Hearty Tomato-Vegetable Soup

A hot and hearty soup, almost a meal in itself.

> *1 10½-ounce can cream of tomato soup*
> *1¼ cups milk*
> *½ cup cooked mixed vegetables (left from dinner)*
> *2 strips crisp fried bacon, crumbled*

Combine soup, milk, and vegetables in a saucepan. Heat, stirring occasionally. Serve topped with crisp bacon croutons. Makes 2 main-dish servings.

Ambrosia

> 1 orange, peeled and sliced
> 1 banana, sliced
> 1 tablespoon sugar
> 2 tablespoons shredded coconut

Half an hour before supper, combine all ingredients and chill. Makes 2 servings.

Braised Lamb Shanks with Fluffy Rice

> 2 tablespoons flour
> ½ teaspoon salt
> ⅛ teaspoon pepper
> 2 lamb shanks (about 1 pound)
> 2 tablespoons shortening
> 1 small onion
> 1 cup water
> 1 10½-ounce can beef bouillon
>   or 1 bouillon cube and 1¼ cups water
> ½ cup raw rice

Combine flour, salt and pepper. Roll shanks in flour mixture, coating well. Heat shortening in a Dutch oven or kettle with tight-fitting cover. Brown shanks in hot fat over low heat, turning to brown well on all sides. Peel and dice onion. Add it together with the water to shanks. Cover and cook slowly for 1¼ hours. While shanks cook set portable kitchen timer as a reminder. Then relax. If leaving the kitchen area, take timer along as a reminder.

In 1¼ hours water on shanks should be almost gone. Add bouillon or bouillon cube and water. Bring to a boil. Add rice.

Turn heat low. Cover and simmer for about 25 minutes or until moisture is absorbed and rice is fluffy and tender. Makes 2 servings plus ½ cup of rice for soup at suppertime.

Five Minute Peach Melba

> 2 *canned peach halves*
> 1 *coarsely crumbled graham cracker*
> 2 *tablespoons raspberry jelly*
> 1 *teaspoon lemon juice*
> 2 *marshmallows*

Heat oven or table baker to 400°F. (moderately hot). Arrange peach halves, rounded side down, in a pie pan or small shallow dish. Blend together cracker crumbs, jelly, and lemon juice. Fill peach halves with this mixture. Top each with a marshmallow. Bake in preheated oven 3 to 4 minutes or until marshmallow is lightly browned. Turn off heat and keep warm during dinner. Makes 2 servings.

Crunchy Topped Gingerbread with Applesauce

> ½ *package gingerbread mix*
> 1 *tablespoon brown sugar*
> 1 *teaspoon flour*
> 1 *teaspoon soft butter or margarine*
> 1 *tablespoon broken walnut meats*

Heat oven to 350°F. (moderate). Prepare the ½ package gingerbread mix, using half of the liquid called for in package directions. Pour batter into 4 greased custard cups. Combine the brown sugar, flour, butter, and nuts. Sprinkle this mixture over the batter in 2 of the custard cups. Bake all four in preheated oven for 20 minutes or until firm to the touch. Serve the 2 Crunchy Topped cupcakes with applesauce. Save the others for Gingerbread-Banana Shortcakes* next day.

Meat Loaf for Two

> ½ pound ground lean beef
> ¼ pound ground veal
> 1 small finely chopped onion
> 2 tablespoons chopped parsley or 1 teaspoon parsley flakes
> ½ teaspoon salt
> ⅛ teaspoon pepper
> ¼ teaspoon crushed sage
> 3 slices soft bread, cut into small cubes
> ⅓ cup milk
> 1 egg, beaten

Mix meats thoroughly. Add remaining ingredients and blend well. Heat oven to 350°F. (moderate). Shape meat mixture into a loaf and place it in a greased, shallow baking pan. Bake in preheated oven for 45 to 50 minutes. Makes 4 servings— two to serve hot with pan drippings for gravy and two to use the next day in sandwiches.

Creamed Chopped Spinach

Cook ½ package frozen spinach as package directs, or cook 1 pound fresh spinach. Drain it, reserving liquid. Quickly bring the juice from the spinach to a boil and cook it until the liquid is reduced to about ¼ cup. Meanwhile, blend together ⅓ cup light cream or milk, 2 teaspoons flour, ¼ teaspoon salt. Stir flour mixture into spinach juice in pan. Add drained spinach and cook over low heat, stirring frequently until bubbling hot and slightly thickened. Serve, if desired, with a wedge of lemon. Makes 2 servings.

Gingerbread-Banana Shortcake

> 2 custard cup Gingerbreads (see Crunchy Topped
>   Gingerbread*)
> 1 ripe banana
> Whipped cream or light cream

Split gingerbread cupcakes crosswise. Slice half of the banana on each bottom layer. Put top of gingerbread back in place. Serve with whipped cream or light cream, whichever you have on hand or like best, or serve with Quick Custard Sauce*, used with Fruit Jello.

Scrambled Eggs with Chipped Beef and Mushrooms

> 1 2½-ounce jar chipped beef
> 2 teaspoons butter or margarine
> 1 teaspoon flour
> 1 3-ounce can mushrooms, stems and pieces
> 2 to 4 buttered, toasted corn muffins

Cut beef into bits. Set aside. Heat butter or margarine in an 8-inch skillet. Blend in flour, then mushrooms, juice and all. Cook slowly, stirring constantly, until sauce is thickened. Beat eggs slightly. Add beef bits and stir into mushrooms. Cook slowly, stirring and scraping the eggs from the bottom and sides of the pan until they are "set" just firm enough to suit you. Serve on the buttered, toasted corn muffins. Makes 2 generous servings.

Quick Custard Sauce for Fruit Jello or Other Desserts

Prepare 1 package of vanilla pudding mix (not instant) as package directs. Chill. For custard sauce for two, thin ½ of the vanilla pudding with ½ cup light cream or milk. Beat it smooth. Pour the unthinned half of the pudding into a bowl and chill to use topped with fruits or chocolate sauce another day.

Homemade Graham Brownies

As you'll see, these brownies almost bake themselves. No sifting, no creaming, no melting of chocolate squares.

>   *1 14-ounce can sweetened condensed milk*
>   *2 cups packaged graham cracker crumbs*
>   *1 cup chopped nut meats (1 4-ounce can)*
>   *1 teaspoon vanilla*
>   *1 teaspoon salt*
>   *1½ cups semisweet chocolate bits*

Heat oven to 350°F. (moderate). Blend together all ingredients. Turn into greased, 9-inch square cake pan. Bake in preheated oven for 30 minutes. Cool on a wire cake rack. Cut, when cool, into squares. Makes 16. They keep and keep, fresh as ever, if covered tightly or wrapped in foil.

Shepherd's Pie for Two

Topped with a fluffy border of whipped potatoes quickly prepared from instant potato flakes, this treat for a twosome turns any winter meal into a special event.

> ½ pound boned shoulder of lamb
> 2 teaspoons salad oil or other fat
> 1 tablespoon minced onion
> 1 tablespoon flour
> Dash pepper
> ½ teaspoon salt
> 1 cup boiling water
> 1 bay leaf (optional)
> 2 carrots, scraped and diced
> 2 to 3 green onions, thinly sliced, tops and all
> Instant whipped potatoes
> 1 teaspoon melted butter or margarine

Remove any gristle from lamb. Heat fat in a Dutch oven. Add onion and cook 1 to 2 minutes. Combine flour, pepper, and salt in a pie pan and roll lamb in flour mixture to coat it well. Brown lamb in hot fat in Dutch oven, turning to brown all sides. Add boiling water and bay leaf. Cover and simmer for 1 hour. Add carrots and green onions. Cover again and continue to cook until vegetables are tender—10 to 12 minutes. Remove bay leaf. Pour meat and vegetables into a greased 1-quart casserole. Heat oven to 425°F. (moderately hot oven). Prepare instant whipped potatoes as package directs for 2 servings. Spoon them in a border around the edge of the casserole. Drizzle with the melted butter and bake in preheated oven for 7 to 10 minutes, or until potato border is beginning to brown lightly. Makes 2 servings.

Refrigerator Pudding

Serve 2 of these custard-cup puddings for dinner dessert and let the extra one double as a shared bedtime snack.

6 packaged vanilla wafers
1 tablespoon raspberry jelly
1 package instant vanilla pudding mix
1½ cups milk

Spread the vanilla wafers with the jelly. Place 1 spread wafer in the bottom of each of 3 custard cups. Blend together the pudding and milk, beating as package directs. Pour ⅓ of the pudding into each custard cup. Let stand 1 minute. Top each with 1 of the remaining spread wafers. Chill. Makes 3 servings.

Broiled Meat Loaf, Tomato, and Cheese Sandwich

1 teaspoon butter or margarine
½ teaspoon bottled horse-radish or prepared mustard
2 to 3 slices bread
2 to 3 slices meat loaf, thinly sliced
4 to 6 thin slices tomato
¼ cup grated American or Cheddar cheese

Heat broiler. Combine butter and horse-radish or mustard. Spread bread lightly with butter mixture. Arrange slices of meat loaf and tomatoes over bread. Sprinkle the grated cheese over the top of each open sandwich. Broil 5 inches from heat until cheese melts (about 3 to 4 minutes).

Or, if you prefer to oven-bake the sandwiches: Heat oven to 450°F. (hot oven). Prepare sandwiches as above and place them on a cookie sheet. Bake them in preheated oven until cheese melts (about 7 to 8 minutes). Makes 2 to 3 sandwiches, or 1 each with an extra half-sandwich dividend.

Swiss Steak for Two

> ½ to ¾ pound round steak cut 1 inch thick
> 1 tablespoon flour
> ¼ teaspoon salt
> Dash pepper
> 1 tablespoon salad oil or melted fat
> ¾ cup tomato juice or canned bouillon
> 1 large onion, thinly sliced
> 1 teaspoon Worcestershire sauce

Trim any excess fat from meat. Combine flour, salt, and pepper. Lay beef on a bread board and pound half of the flour mixture into it with the rim of a heavy saucer. Turn meat and pound the rest of the flour into the other side. Heat the salad oil or fat in a Dutch oven over medium heat. Brown meat well on both sides. Add the rest of the ingredients. Set the timer for 45 minutes. Cover and simmer steak until timer rings. Forty-five minutes to water the plants, write a letter, or just relax! Then "peek" and add more tomato juice or bouillon, if necessary, to keep about 1 inch of liquid bubbling around the steak. Cover again. Set timer for 30 minutes. Serve piping hot. You'll find it is almost fork-tender, juicy with its own gravy. Makes 2 servings.

Tangy Carrot and Celery Slaw

> 1 medium-sized raw carrot
> 1 large stalk celery
> Dash onion salt
> ¼ teaspoon dill seeds (optional)
> 1 tablespoon catsup
> 1 to 2 tablespoons mayonnaise

Scrape carrot and grate it on a medium grater. Wash, dry, and slice celery thinly. Combine all ingredients, tossing lightly with a fork. Chill. Serve on crisp greens—lettuce, chicory, or even tiny crisp raw spinach leaves. Makes 2 servings.

Apricot Sauce

This sauce, made in less time than it takes to tell, turns packaged sponge cups, filled with ice cream, into a special treat.

> *2 tablespoons sugar*
> *1 teaspoon cornstarch*
> *⅔ cup canned apricot juice*
>   *(or juice saved from drained stewed dried apricots)*
> *¼ teaspoon grated lemon rind (optional, but nice)*
> *1 tablespoon fresh or bottled lemon juice*
> *2 whole cloves or a dash of nutmeg*

Combine sugar and cornstarch in a small saucepan. Slowly stir in apricot juice, lemon rind, lemon juice, and cloves or nutmeg. Quickly bring the mixture to a boil. Reduce heat and cook over low heat, stirring constantly until clear and slightly thickened—about 2 minutes. Cool, cover, and chill. Makes sauce for 2 sponge cups filled with ice cream, or for many other puddings such as custard, Jello, etc.

Deviled Ham French Toast

> *2 eggs*
> *¼ teaspoon salt*
> *2 teaspoons sugar*
> *3 tablespoons milk*
> *2 tablespoons canned deviled ham*
> *4 slices enriched bread*
> *2 teaspoons butter or margarine*
> *Apple butter or syrup*

Break eggs into a pie pan. Beat them slightly with a fork. Stir in salt, sugar, milk and deviled ham. Blend well.

Heat butter or margarine in a skillet. Quickly dip bread slices into egg mixture, one at a time, turning to coat each side. Brown them on both sides in the skillet, turning once. Serve with apple butter or syrup. Makes 2 slices each for 2.

Escalloped Macaroni and Tuna

> 2 eggs
> 1 cup cooked macaroni (½ cup uncooked)
> 2 tablespoons chopped pimiento
> 1 10½-ounce can cream of celery soup (undiluted)
> 1 teaspoon instant onion or 2 teaspoons minced onion
> 1 3½-ounce can tuna
> ½ cup packaged grated American cheese

Heat oven to 325°F. (moderately slow oven). Beat eggs in a medium-sized bowl. Stir in macaroni, pimiento, celery soup, and onion. Flake tuna with a fork and add. Stir in half of cheese. Grease a 1-quart casserole. Pour macaroni mixture into it and sprinkle the rest of the cheese over the top. Set the casserole in a larger pan. Pour hot water around it to within 1 inch of the top. Bake in preheated oven for 1 hour. Makes 2 generous main-dish servings.

Butterscotch Graham Cracker Pudding

> 1 teaspoon sugar
> 2 tablespoons packaged graham cracker crumbs
> 1½ cups milk
> 1 package butterscotch-flavored instant pudding
> 1 tablespoon chopped walnut meats (optional)

Blend together the sugar and crumbs. Pour the milk into a bowl and add the pudding mix. Beat with an egg beater for 1 minute. Spoon half of the crumb mixture into 3 custard cups. Fill cups with pudding mixture. Sprinkle the remaining crumbs over the top of the pudding. (Pudding will still be liquid, so let stand 2 minutes, or until thickened before moving to the refrigerator.) Chill. Makes 3 puddings, two for dessert and one to divide as a bedtime snack.

Shrimp and Corn Bisque

> 1 10-ounce can frozen cream of shrimp soup
> 1 4¾-ounce jar strained corn
> 1 teaspoon minced onion
>   or ½ teaspoon instant onion
> ⅛ teaspoon leaf thyme (optional)
> ¾ cup milk

Remove frozen soup from freezing compartment and let it stand in a pan of hot water for a few minutes. Open soup and it will slide out easily into a saucepan. Add the rest of the ingredients and heat very slowly until steaming hot. Makes 2 main-dish servings.

Heavenly Hash

Remember this old favorite? Sometimes made with drained crushed pineapple instead of dried apricots, it is a tasty nutritious dessert either way. Serve it often when you have ½ cup leftover rice.

12 dried apricot halves
½ cup cooked rice
6 marshmallows or
     ⅔ cup miniature marshmallows
1 teaspoon sugar
⅓ cup heavy cream, whipped
1 to 2 tablespoons juice drained from apricots

In a small saucepan combine apricots and just enough boiling water to cover them. Simmer apricots for 10 minutes. Cool and drain. Cut the apricots into bits and stir them into the rice. Snip the marshmallows into bits, too. A kitchen scissors works well for snipping both apricots and marshmallows. Add marshmallow bits and remaining ingredients to rice and apricots. Toss lightly with a fork to blend. Chill. Makes 2 servings.

Creamy Rice Custard

You may have a yearning for this old, old favorite. If so, serve it instead of Heavenly Hash.* Start it baking at dinnertime while Escalloped Macaroni and Tuna* bakes. Then chill it until suppertime.

2 eggs
⅓ cup cooked rice
Dash salt
1 teaspoon vanilla extract
¼ cup seedless raisins (optional)
½ teaspoon grated lemon rind
1¾ cups milk (or use half evaporated milk and half
     water)
1 tablespoon butter or margarine

Grease a 1-quart casserole. Heat oven to 325°F. (same temperature as for the tuna casserole). Beat eggs and stir in the remaining ingredients. Pour into the casserole. Set casserole into a larger baking pan and fill pan with hot water to 1 inch from the top of the casserole. Bake until a silver knife, inserted in the center, comes out clean (about 1 hour). Cool at room temperature, then chill. Makes 2 to 3 servings.

Cinnamon Tea

For an after-dinner "snifter" nothing can beat this hot spicy soother, especially if the wind blows cold outside. It is good to serve, too, if someone drops in, looking just about too cold to be happy.

> 2 cups water
> 1 stick cinnamon (2 inches long)
> 4 to 5 whole cloves
> 2 tea bags

Combine water, stick cinnamon, and cloves in a small saucepan. Very slowly heat the brew to boiling. Pour over the tea bags and steep for 3 minutes. Strain and serve with sugar and lemon if desired.

Baked Chicken with Fluffy Onion Rice

> 2 chicken legs or 1 double breast, split
> 1 tablespoon flour
> ½ teaspoon salt
> ⅛ teaspoon pepper
> 2 tablespoons shortening or bacon drippings
> ⅔ cup raw rice
> ½ package dry onion soup mix
> 2 cups boiling water

Choose dark or light parts of chicken to suit yourself. Blend together flour, salt, and pepper in a brown paper bag or in a pie pan. Shake or roll chicken parts in flour mixture to coat them well. Heat shortening in a skillet and brown chicken over low heat in the hot fat, turning to brown it evenly on both sides. Heat the oven to 375°F. (moderately hot oven). Measure rice into a 1½-quart casserole with a cover (or the baking dish may be covered with aluminum foil). Pour all of onion soup mix into a small bowl and stir it to blend thoroughly. Measure half of it back into its container and save it for 2 cups of hot onion soup at another meal. Stir half of the soup mix and the boiling water into the rice. (Don't salt the rice. The onion soup gives just enough seasoning). Lay browned chicken pieces on top of rice. Cover and bake in preheated oven for 45 minutes. Uncover and continue to bake until rice and chicken are very tender, about 10 minutes longer. Makes 2 generous servings.

Vegetable Omelet

Use up refrigerated bits of this and that within a few days. Here is an easy, tasty way to do it. No matter whether those leftover dabs are cooked vegetables, cooked rice, bits of ham, let them add flavor and nutrition to an omelet.

2 tablespoons butter or margarine
3 eggs
3 tablespoons milk
¼ teaspoon salt
Dash paprika
½ cup cooked vegetables or minced, cooked meat

Heat butter or margarine in an 8-inch skillet over low heat. Beat the eggs well and stir in the remaining ingredients. Pour into hot fat in the pan and cook over low heat. As the mixture "sets" at the edges, gently lift up the firm edges with a spatula, tilting the pan to let the raw mixture pour under to the bottom of the pan. When the omelet is almost firm, turn off the heat and cover the pan for 1 minute. Then fold the omelet in half and roll it out onto a heated serving platter. Makes 2 servings.

Baked-Ahead Cheese-Glazed Apples

Bake these at noon along with the Baked Chicken with Fluffy Onion Rice.* Then supper will almost get itself.

> 2 large, firm baking apples
> 1/3 cup sugar
> 1/4 teaspoon cinnamon
> 1 tablespoon seedless raisins (optional)
> 1/2 teaspoon grated orange rind
> 1/2 cup orange juice
> 2 to 3 tablespoons grated American cheese

Heat oven to 375°F. (moderately hot oven). Wash and core apples. Place them in a small, shallow baking dish. Combine 1 tablespoon of the sugar with the cinnamon and sprinkle the mixture into the holes where cores were removed. Fill holes with the raisins. Combine the remaining sugar, rind, and juice. Pour this juice mixture over and around the apples. Cover, using aluminum foil if necessary, and bake for 30 minutes, along with the chicken casserole. Uncover, sprinkle with grated cheese, and continue to bake until the apples are puffed and fork-tender, the cheese melted (about 15 minutes uncovered). Cool. Then cover at room temperature and serve at suppertime. Makes 2 servings.

Spring

MENUS AND RECIPES

Did it seem that spring would never come? Now, all of a sudden, a green mist shows on the trees and, at last, the weather lets you enjoy a walk. You can't wait to get the potted plants outside or to putter a bit in the garden!

Don't deny yourself these outdoor pleasures just because you have a dinner to prepare. Let dinner cook by itself while you are outdoors working up an appetite. With a kitchen timer-clock in your pocket or ticking away on a nearby stool or fence post, you won't forget foods baking or boiling that might otherwise cook too long.

MENUS

SUNDAY

BREAKFAST

Orange and Pineapple Juice
Ready-to-Eat Cereal
Crisp Bacon
Buttered Toast
Glass of Milk
Coffee or Tea

DINNER

*Roast Stuffed Breast of Lamb with Apple Mint Jelly
Small Roasted Canned Potatoes
*Sweet and Sour New Beet Greens
*Carrot and Raisin Salad
Rolls   Butter or Margarine
Lemon Sherbet   Packaged Cookies
Tea or Coffee (optional)

SUPPER

*Cracker Barrel Omelet
Leaf Lettuce   *Sour Cream Dressing
Packaged Corn Muffins   Honey
*Red Cinnamon Rhubarb Sauce
Cookies
Glass of Milk
Tea or Coffee (optional)

MONDAY

BREAKFAST

Sliced Bananas with Cream
*Jelly Roll French Toast
Glass of Milk
Coffee or Tea

DINNER

Small Glass of Grapefruit Juice
*Skillet Pork Chop Dinner
*Pear and Stuffed Prune Salad
Chocolate Pudding
Half Glass of Milk
Tea or Coffee (optional)

SUPPER

Cream of Vegetable Soup with a Dash of Curry Powder
*Grilled Cheese Dreams with Crisp Bacon
Fruit Jello with Quick Custard Sauce* or Light Cream
Packaged Cookies
Half Glass of Milk
Tea or Coffee (optional)

TUESDAY

BREAKFAST

Small Glass of Prune Juice
Quick-Cooking Cereal
Scrambled Eggs
Toast
Half Glass of Milk
Coffee or Tea

DINNER

Cup of Hot Tomato Juice
*Chicken Diva
Instant Mashed Potatoes
*Wilted Fresh Spinach or
Hearts of Lettuce   Russian Dressing
Packaged Refrigerator Biscuits
Butter or Margarine   Jelly
Compote of Canned Fruits
Cookies
Glass of Milk
Tea or Coffee (optional)

SUPPER

*Vegetable Rabbit on English Muffins or
Chicken Salad Sandwiches
Celery Sticks   Olives
*Rhubarb and Strawberry Delight
Packaged Cupcakes
Half Glass of Milk
Tea or Coffee (optional)

WEDNESDAY

BREAKFAST

Orange Juice
*Poached Eggs on Deviled Ham Toast
Glass of Milk
Coffee or Tea

DINNER

Browned Lamburgers with Creamed Asparagus
Parsley Buttered New Potatoes
Grated Apple and Carrot Slaw
Bread   Butter or Margarine
Sliced Red-Ripe Strawberries with Cream
Glass of Milk
Tea or Coffee (optional)

SUPPER

*Cheese Puff
*Tomato and Vegetable Aspic
Bread   Butter or Margarine
Canned Peach Halves
Cinnamon Graham Crackers
Half Glass of Milk
Tea or Coffee (optional)

THURSDAY

BREAKFAST

Half Grapefruit or Canned Grapefruit Segments
Quick-Cooking Cereal
Coffeecake
Crisp Bacon (optional)
Glass of Milk
Coffee or Tea

DINNER

*Barbecued Spring Chicken
*Buttered New Potatoes and Peas in Cream
Finely Grated New Cabbage Slaw
Bread   Butter or Margarine
Canned Whole Apricots   Packaged Macaroons
or Butterscotch Pudding
Half Glass of Milk
Tea or Coffee (optional)

SUPPER

Cup of Chicken Consommé with Rice
*Chicken Hodgepodge Salad
Bread   Butter or Margarine
Packaged Marble Cake Slices with Green Applesauce
Glass of Milk

FRIDAY

BREAKFAST

Apricot Nectar
Soft-Cooked Eggs
Toast   Marmalade
Glass of Milk
Tea or Coffee

DINNER

*Fish Fillet Rolls with Chives
Steamed Rice
Buttered New Carrots or Turnips
Shredded Chinese Cabbage   Thousand Island Dressing
Bread   Butter or Margarine
*Jiffy Lemon-Grape-Nuts Refrigerator Pudding
Glass of Milk
Tea or Coffee (optional)

SUPPER

Grilled Tuna Salad Sandwiches
Pear Salad
*Honey Cup Custard
Glass of Milk or Hot Chocolate

SATURDAY

BREAKFAST

Pineapple Juice
Quick-Cooking Cereal
Packaged Heat-and-Serve Sausages
Toast   Honey
Glass of Milk
Tea or Coffee

DINNER

*Baked Stuffed Franks
Frozen Potato Patties
Snap Beans with Parsley Butter
Bread   Butter or Margarine
Crisp New Carrot Sticks   Pickles
*Strawberry Pudding Parfait
Milk
Tea or Coffee (optional)

SUPPER

*Potatoes au Gratin with Poached Eggs
Spring Salad Greens   French Dressing
Green Applesauce
Packaged Cookies
Glass of Milk
Tea or Coffee (optional)

Roast Stuffed Breast of Lamb

Don't think that a 1½ pound breast of lamb is too much for two people. It is just about right, because there is a good bit of bone. Your 1½ pound breast of lamb will be about the least expensive meat you can buy. This roast, worthy of a Sunday-dinner menu, will be startlingly inexpensive.

> *1 breast of lamb (about 1½ pounds)*
> *½ teaspoon salt*
> *¼ teaspoon pepper*
> *½ package stuffing mix*
> *1 small onion, minced*
> *4 tablespoons butter or margarine*
> *¼ cup water*

Have your butcher cut a pocket in the lamb for the stuffing. Also ask him for several wooden skewers. Sprinkle the inside of the pocket with salt and pepper. In a small saucepan combine the onion, butter, and water. Bring to a boil. Pour over stuffing in a bowl and toss to blend well. Stuff it into the pocket in the lamb. Insert wooden skewers across the opening and lace it partly closed with twine. Heat oven to 350°F. (moderate oven). Place the roast in a shallow roasting pan and roast it for 1 hour, or until nicely browned. Serve piping hot with apple mint jelly. Makes 2 servings.

Sweet and Sour New Beet Greens

1 pound beet greens
1 slice bacon
1 scallion, cut in thin slices, tops and all
1 tablespoon sugar
⅛ teaspoon salt
⅛ teaspoon pepper
2 tablespoons vinegar

Wash greens well. Let them stand in cold water for another rinsing while you are at church. Then drain them. Ten minutes before dinnertime start cooking greens in boiling, salted water to cover. Cook for 5 minutes. Drain well. Meanwhile, fry bacon crisp and crumble it into bits. To bacon fat in pan add scallion, sugar, salt, pepper, and vinegar. Bring to a boil and simmer for 1 minute. Pour over beet greens. Sprinkle with bacon bits. Makes 2 servings.

Carrot and Raisin Salad

¼ cup seedless raisins
1 small carrot
2 tablespoons mayonnaise
⅛ teaspoon salt
⅛ teaspoon pepper
Crisp Spring greens

Measure raisins into a bowl. Scrape carrot and grate it into the bowl with the raisins. Add mayonnaise, salt and pepper. Toss to blend. Serve on crisp greens. Makes 2 servings.

Cracker Barrel Omelet

> *4 eggs*
> *1 teaspoon cold water*
> *½ teaspoon salt*
> *Speck pepper*
> *½ cup crushed saltine-type crackers*
> *1 tablespoon butter or margarine*

Break the eggs into a bowl and beat them well with an egg beater. Add cold water, salt, and pepper. Crush the crackers into a measuring cup. Heat the butter or margarine in a small- to medium-sized skillet. Sprinkle in the cracker crumbs. Pour in the eggs. Turn heat low. As the eggs "set" at the edges, gently lift them with a spatula and tip the pan so that the uncooked egg mixture pours down under the edges. When eggs are almost firm turn off the heat and cover the pan for 1 minute. Then loosen the edges of the omelet all around with a spatula and fold it in half. Roll out onto a heated platter. Serve crisp, crusted omelet with chili sauce, if you like. Makes 2 servings.

Sour Cream Dressing for Leaf Lettuce

> *1 tablespoon sugar*
> *2 tablespoons vinegar*
> *Dash salt*
> *⅓ cup commercial sour cream*
> *2 cups well-washed, drained leaf lettuce*

Stir sugar, vinegar, and salt into sour cream. Toss dressing through leaf lettuce. Makes 2 servings.

Red Cinnamon Rhubarb Sauce

> *¾ pound rhubarb*
> *¼ cup water*
> *Dash salt*
> *2 tablespoons sugar*
> *½ cup red cinnamon candy drops*

Wash rhubarb; discard root and leaf ends. Cut stalks into 1-inch pieces, without peeling. Combine all ingredients in a saucepan. Cover and simmer for 10 minutes, or until tender, stirring once or twice. Chill. Makes 2 servings.

Jelly Roll French Toast

> *1 egg*
> *Dash salt*
> *1 teaspoon sugar*
> *2 tablespoons milk*
> *Butter or margarine*
> *3 to 4 slices enriched bread, thin sliced*
> *4 teaspoons raspberry, currant, or strawberry jelly*

Break egg into a pie pan. Beat it lightly with a fork. Stir in salt, sugar, and milk. Heat a little butter or margarine in a skillet. Quickly dip the bread slices into the egg mixture, one at a time. Turn them to coat on both sides. Remove them at once to the skillet. Brown both sides, turning once. Spread each slice with jelly and roll up. Serve 2 slices each. Makes 2 servings.

Skillet Pork Chop Dinner

> *2 to 3 pork chops (about 12 ounces)*
> *⅔ cup canned cream of vegetable soup*
> *½ cup water*
> *2 to 3 rings of green pepper*
> *2 to 3 slices tomato*
> *⅓ cup raw rice*

Brown chops in a heavy skillet with tight-fitting cover or in a Dutch oven. Turn to brown both sides. Drain off fat. Pour soup and water around chops; cover and cook over low heat for 20 minutes. Stir in rice. Arrange a green pepper ring and a slice of tomato on each chop. Cover and continue to cook slowly for 25 to 30 minutes, or until rice is tender. Peek once during the last ten minutes and if rice is beginning to stick, add ¼ cup more water. Makes 2 generous servings—one chop each and one more for the hungrier.

Pear and Stuffed Prune Salad

> *2 stewed prunes, drained*
> *2 tablespoons cream cheese*
> *1 tablespoon peanut butter*
> *2 well-drained, chilled canned pear halves*
> *Crisp greens*
> *French dressing*

Remove the pits from the prunes. Blend together the cream cheese and peanut butter. Fill holes where pit was removed with peanut butter mixture. Arrange pear halves on greens, rounded sides down. Place stuffed prunes on pear halves. Serve on greens with French dressing.

Grilled Cheese Dreams with Crisp Bacon

4 slices enriched bread
1 teaspoon prepared mustard
4 slices packaged American cheese
2 tablespoons butter or margarine
Chili sauce or catsup
Crisp fried bacon slices

Spread 2 slices of the bread lightly with mustard. Then place 2 slices of cheese on each. Top the cheese with the two remaining bread slices. Heat butter or margarine in a skillet and fry the sandwiches, turning to brown lightly on both sides. Serve with chili sauce or catsup, as desired, and with crisp bacon slices. Makes 2 sandwiches.

If you prefer, use your automatic sandwich toaster. Spread the outside surfaces of the sandwiches with the butter or margarine. Heat grill and arrange sandwiches on one surface. Close grill for 3 to 4 minutes, or until sandwiches are nicely browned.

Chicken Diva

½ pound fresh asparagus or
*   1 10½-ounce can asparagus spears*
½ of a 6½-ounce can boneless chicken
⅔ cup cream of mushroom soup
2 tablespoons milk
¼ package grated American cheese

Clean fresh asparagus. Cut off about 2 inches of the tough stalk ends. Save for creamed asparagus another day.

Cook asparagus for 5 minutes. Drain. (Or use canned.) Heat oven to 450°F. (hot). Arrange asparagus in a shallow baking dish or pie pan. Top it with the chicken. Blend the soup and milk; pour over chicken. Sprinkle with the cheese and bake in preheated oven until lightly browned on top and bubbling hot—about 15 minutes. Makes 3 servings, or one each with small "seconds" for both.

Wilted Fresh Spinach

1 pound fresh spinach
1 slice bacon
2 teaspoons sugar
¼ teaspoon salt
3 tablespoons vinegar
1 tablespoon chopped pimiento (optional)
1 scallion, tops and all, sliced

Wash spinach well. Drain. Fry bacon crisp. Drain it on a paper towel, then crumble it into bits. To the bacon drippings in the pan add the remaining ingredients. Bring to a boil and simmer for 1 minute. Pour over spinach, tossing to coat each leaf. Sprinkle with bacon bits. Makes 2 servings.

Vegetable Rabbit on English Muffins

1 tablespoon butter or margarine
1 tablespoon flour
¼ teaspoon salt
¼ teaspoon dry mustard
¾ cup milk
½ cup packaged grated sharp cheese
1 cup leftover cooked vegetables
2 toasted, buttered English muffins

Melt butter in a small saucepan. Add flour, salt, and mustard. Blend in milk. Stir over low heat until thick and smooth. Add cheese and vegetables, stirring until cheese is melted. Serve over toasted, buttered English muffins. Makes 2 servings.

Rhubarb and Strawberry Delight

> ½ pound fresh rhubarb
> 2 tablespoons water
> ⅓ cup sugar
> ¼ cup strawberry preserves

Wash rhubarb and cut it into 1-inch pieces. Add water and simmer until almost tender, about 5 minutes, stirring once or twice. Add sugar and cook for 1 more minute. Stir in preserves. Pour into individual sauce dishes and chill.

Poached Egg on Deviled Ham Toast

> 2 eggs
> 2 slices toast
> 2 tablespoons canned deviled ham

Grease a small skillet. Add 2 cups water and ¼ teaspoon salt. Heat to boiling. Turn heat low and break the eggs, one at a time, into a custard cup. Carefully slide them into the simmering water. Cook for 3 minutes or until eggs are "set" enough to suit you. Meanwhile, make toast and spread it with the deviled ham. With a slotted spoon, remove the eggs from the pan to the ham-spread toast. Makes 2 servings.

Browned Lamburgers with Creamed Asparagus

Fresh asparagus belongs to spring as perhaps no other food quite does. It isn't here long, so serve it while you can. When preparing it for a vegetable, cut off about 2 inches of the coarse ends, scrape them, and save for creamed sauces to serve like this, with meats.

> *Stalk ends, cut from ½ pound fresh asparagus*
>   *(about ⅔ cup cleaned and diced)*
> *½ pound ground lean lamb*
> *¼ teaspoon salt*
> *⅛ teaspoon pepper*
> *2 teaspoons catsup*
> *1 tablespoon shortening*
> *2 teaspoons flour*
> *Dash salt*
> *½ cup milk*

Cook cut-up asparagus in boiling salted water until tender, about 8 minutes. Drain. Combine lamb, salt, pepper, and catsup. Form into 2 patties. Heat fat in a small skillet and brown the patties on both sides. Cover skillet and cook for 5 minutes. Remove patties to hot serving plates while making sauce. Stir flour and salt into the fat in the pan. Slowly stir in the milk and cook over low heat, stirring, until bubbling and thickened. Add asparagus. Serve over lamb patties. Makes 2 servings.

Cheese Puff

This proud and puffy soufflé looks to be bigger than it is. Really the two of you can finish it, since the rest of the supper is rather light.

⅔ cup cream of mushroom soup
½ cup grated sharp cheese
3 eggs, separated

Heat oven to 300°F. (slow). In a saucepan combine the soup and cheese. Heat slowly, stirring occasionally, until the cheese melts. Remove from heat. Beat the egg yolks well and stir them into the soup mixture. Then beat the whites stiff. Fold the soup mixture into the stiff whites. Pour into an ungreased 1-quart baking dish and bake in preheated oven for 1 hour. Makes 2 to 3 servings.

Tomato and Vegetable Aspic

¾ cup tomato juice
1 teaspoon unflavored gelatin
½ teaspoon instant minced onion
⅓ cup grated raw carrot
Crisp lettuce leaves or spring greens
Mayonnaise

Pour about 2 tablespoons of the tomato juice into a custard cup and the rest of it into a small saucepan. Sprinkle the gelatin over the juice in the cup. Heat the juice in the pan with the instant onion until it begins to simmer. Remove from heat and stir in the softened gelatin, stirring until gelatin is dissolved. Spoon half of the grated carrot into each of 2 custard cups or 4-ounce individual molds. Pour the hot juice over the carrot layers and chill until firm, about 1½ hours. Unmold onto greens and serve with mayonnaise. Makes 2 servings.

Barbecued Spring Chicken

> ½ of a 2 or 2½ pound frying chicken,
>   cut in two pieces
> 1 tablespoon flour
> ¼ teaspoon salt
> ¼ teaspoon paprika
> 1 tablespoon shortening
> ⅓ cup catsup
> ⅓ cup water
> 1 teaspoon instant minced onion
> 2 teaspoons chopped parsley

Wash and dry the chicken pieces. In a clean paper bag combine flour, salt, and paprika. Shake the chicken in the flour mixture to coat it well. Heat the shortening in a skillet with a cover, or in a Dutch oven. Brown the chicken slowly in the fat, turning to brown all sides. Combine the catsup, water, onion, and parsley. Pour over the chicken. Cover and cook slowly for 30 minutes or until tender, adding a bit more water from time to time if necessary to keep chicken from sticking. Makes 2 servings.

Buttered New Potatoes and Peas in Cream

> 4 small new potatoes
> 1 cup shelled fresh peas or ½ package frozen peas
> ⅛ teaspoon salt
> ¼ cup light cream

Scrub potatoes and scrape them. Cook until almost tender in boiling, salted water. Add the peas and continue to cook until potatoes and peas are tender. Drain. Heat salt and cream and pour over the potatoes. Makes 2 servings.

Chicken Hodgepodge Salad

Guaranteed to use refrigerator dabs to good advantage. Guaranteed as a tasty, hearty supper main dish, too.

> ½ of a 6½-ounce can of boneless chicken, diced, or
> ⅔ cup cooked diced chicken
> ½ cup cooked leftover peas, potatoes, carrots, etc.
> 1 hard-cooked egg, diced (optional)
> 1 tablespoon catsup
> 2 tablespoons mayonnaise
> Dash salt
> Crisp spring greens

Toss together chicken, vegetables, egg, catsup, mayonnaise, and salt. Chill. Serve on crisp greens. Makes 2 supper main-dish salads.

Fish Fillet Rolls with Chives

> 2 thawed frozen or fresh fish fillets (haddock, cod, etc.)
> 1 tablespoon melted butter or margarine
> 1 teaspoon lemon juice
> 2 teaspoons snipped chives
> ¼ teaspoon salt
> 2 teaspoons flour

Heat oven to 400°F. (moderately hot). In a pie pan combine butter or margarine, lemon juice, 1 teaspoon of the chives, and salt. Dip each piece of fish in this mixture, turning to coat both sides well. Roll the fillets up, jelly-roll fashion, and pin them in place with toothpicks. Stand fish rolls in a greased shallow baking dish and spoon the flour over them. Drizzle with the rest of the lemon juice mixture. Bake in preheated oven for 25 to 30 minutes or until fish is easily flaked with a fork. Serve sprinkled with the rest of the chives. Makes 2 servings.

Jiffy Lemon-Grape-Nuts Refrigerator Pudding

1 14-ounce can sweetened condensed milk
2 teaspoons grated lemon rind
½ cup lemon juice
1 well-beaten egg
⅔ cup Grape-Nuts cereal or 4 ladyfingers, split

Blend together in a bowl the condensed milk, lemon rind, lemon juice, and egg. Beat for 1 minute. Pour half of the pudding into a serving dish (2 to 2½ cups capacity). Sprinkle half of the cereal over, or top with half the ladyfingers. Repeat. Chill for at least 2 hours. Makes 3 to 4 servings. It won't go begging. Chilled in the refrigerator, it keeps for several days.

Honey Cup Custard

2 tablespoons honey
2 cups milk
1 package instant vanilla pudding mix

Measure 1 tablespoon of honey into each of two custard cups. Combine the milk and pudding mix in a bowl. Beat with an egg beater for 1 minute. Ladle pudding over the honey, filling the custard cups. Pour the remaining pudding into a small bowl and save for Strawberry Pudding Parfait* (see Saturday menu).

Baked Stuffed Franks

4 frankfurters (½ pound)
1 cup coarsely crumbled saltine-type crackers
2 strips bacon, cooked crisp
1 teaspoon grated onion
2 tablespoons minced green pepper (optional)
¼ teaspoon salt
Dash pepper
2 tablespoons catsup

Heat oven to 350°F. (moderate). Split franks lengthwise, almost through. Measure cracker crumbs into a bowl. Crumble the bacon and add it, together with the rest of the ingredients, to the crumbs. Toss to blend. Fill the frankfurters with crumb stuffing. Place them in a shallow baking pan. Pour 2 tablespoons of water around them and bake uncovered, in preheated oven, for 15 minutes. Makes 2 servings.

Strawberry Pudding Parfait

Instant vanilla pudding from half a package (see Honey Cup Custard*)
1 cup fresh strawberries, cleaned and sliced
Mint leaves (optional)

Spoon alternate layers of vanilla pudding and chilled strawberries into sherbet glasses or dessert dishes. If you've a bed of mint, garnish puddings with mint sprigs. Makes 2 generous servings.

Potatoes au Gratin with Poached Eggs

> ¾ *cup instant potato flakes or 1½ cups leftover mashed potatoes*
> ¼ *cup grated Cheddar cheese*
> *2 eggs*
> ⅛ *teaspoon salt*
> *Paprika*
> *Parsley flakes*

Prepare the ¾ cup instant potato flakes as package directs. Stir in the grated cheese. Grease a pie pan. Heat the oven to 425°F. (moderately hot). Spoon 2 mounds of potatoes into the pie pan. Make a deep depression in each. Break an egg into each depression and sprinkle with salt, paprika, and parsley. Bake in preheated oven for 12 to 15 minutes, or until eggs are "set." Makes 2 servings.

Chapter Four

SOFT FOODS TEMPORARILY

There are times when even a well person may need soft foods temporarily. Perhaps dental work makes chewing a problem. Perhaps your doctor suggests a soft diet for you or your husband. Keep in mind that preparation and texture of foods are changed, but food requirements are the same. Breakfasts with cooked cereal, eggs, and juices need little change. Toast prepared as milk toast or softened with hot cream will require little effort to chew, and never hesitate for a minute to "dunk" toast. You've a perfect right to. Milk, milk products, soups, cottage cheese, grated cheese, canned fruits, ground meats, fish, and chicken all come into their own to make meals just as adequate as those usually served. Flavor need not be sacrificed either. Seasonings, unless forbidden by the doctor for some reason, are more important than ever.

So here you are with ready-made menus and the recipes you'll need in preparing them, plus a few easily digested bedtime nightcaps to prove that soft foods are tempting and tasty.

MENUS

I

BREAKFAST

Applesauce
*Cinnamon Milk Toast
Tea   Coffee   Hot Chocolate

DINNER

*Creamy Chicken Hash
Packaged Escalloped Potatoes
Stewed Canned Tomatoes
*Caramel Tapioca Pudding
Tea
Glass of Milk

SUPPER

Small Glass of Grapefruit Juice
*Corn Pudding with Ground Ham
Canned Buttered Asparagus Tips
Pear Salad (canned) with Grated Raw Carrot   Mayonnaise
*Floating Island
Tea
Half Glass of Milk

II

A menu that almost prepares itself. Good for a pepless day.

BREAKFAST

Sliced Bananas with Cream
Quick-Cooking Cereal
Poached Egg on Creamy Toast
(Toast Softened with Hot Cream)
Instant Coffee or Tea

DINNER

Grape Juice or Orange Juice (small glass)
*Cheese Custard
Canned Peas in Cream
Peach Halves (canned)
Ladyfingers
Tea
Glass of Milk

SUPPER

*Oyster Milk Toast
Cottage Cheese Salad
Fruit Jello (with canned mixed fruits)
Quick Custard Sauce*
Tea

III

A soft menu to make the grumpiest
"won't eat this" husband beam.

BREAKFAST

Pineapple Juice
*Shirred Eggs with Minced Ham
Quick-Cooking Cereal
Buttered Toast (to be dunked if desired)
Coffee or Tea

DINNER

*Tomato Bouillon
*Baked Chicken with Spanish Rice
Creamed Carrots
*Lemon Sponge Pudding
Glass of Milk
Tea

SUPPER

*Spaghetti Supreme
Buttered Spinach with Lemon Slice
Canned Fruit Compote
Toasted Pound Cake
Tea
Glass of Milk

IV

BREAKFAST

Stewed Dried Apricots
Quick-Cooking Cereal
French Toast   Honey or Syrup
Glass of Milk
Coffee or Tea

DINNER

Cup of Hot Tomato Juice
*Salmon Loaf Supreme
Instant Whipped Potatoes
Bread   Butter or Margarine
Vanilla Pudding with Crushed Pineapple
Half Glass of Milk
Tea

SUPPER

Cream of Mushroom Soup
Crackers and Cream Cheese
Jellied Fruit Salad
Chocolate Chip Ice Cream
Packaged Cupcake
Half Glass of Milk
Tea

Cinnamon Milk Toast (for Two)

1½ cups milk
1 teaspoon butter or margarine
2 to 3 slices buttered toast
2 teaspoons sugar
Dash cinnamon (or 2 teaspoons packaged cinnamon
sugar)

In a small saucepan heat the milk and butter until tiny bubbles begin to form around the edge of the pan. Meanwhile make toast, butter it, and sprinkle with the sugar and cinnamon. Cut slices of toast in half and place half of it in each of two cereal bowls. Pour the hot milk over toast and let it "steep" a minute until softened. Makes 2 servings.

Creamy Chicken Hash

½ cup light cream
½ teaspoon grated lemon rind
1 teaspoon flour
Dash salt
Dash pepper
1 teaspoon grated onion
1 cup coarsely diced cooked chicken
    or 1 6-ounce can boneless chicken
1 tablespoon grated Parmesan cheese

Combine cream, lemon rind, flour, salt, pepper, and onion in a saucepan. Add chicken and cook, stirring, over low heat until sauce bubbles and is slightly thickened. Serve sprinkled with the grated cheese. Makes 2 servings.

Caramel Tapioca Cream

1 egg
3 tablespoons minute tapioca
¼ cup brown sugar, packed
1 teaspoon butter or margarine
⅛ teaspoon salt
¾ cup evaporated milk
¾ cup water (or use 1½ cups milk instead of half evapo-
*   rated milk and half water)*

Beat egg. In a saucepan combine egg and remaining ingredients. Cook over low heat, stirring constantly, until mixture comes to a full boil. Pour into dessert dishes. Serve warm or chilled. Makes 2 to 3 servings.

Corn Pudding with Ground Ham

2 eggs
1¼ cups milk
1 4¾-ounce jar strained creamed corn
¼ teaspoon salt
2 slices boiled ham, diced, or ¼ cup diced baked ham

Heat oven to 325°F. (moderately slow oven). Beat eggs. Add remaining ingredients. Stir to blend. Grease a 1-quart baking dish. Pour mixture into the greased dish. Set it in a larger pan filled with 1 inch of hot water. Bake, uncovered, in preheated oven for 1 hour or until a silver knife, inserted in the center, comes out clean. Serve hot. Makes two main-dish servings.

Floating Island

Almost forgotten today, Floating Island was a turn-of-the-century Sunday or party dessert. Children sometimes called it "floating clouds." Remember?

> ½ package vanilla pudding mix (not the instant)
> 1¼ cups milk or ¾ cup evaporated milk
>   and ½ cup water
> 1 egg
> 2 tablespoons sugar
> Raspberry or currant jelly

Combine the pudding mix and milk in a small saucepan. Cook over low heat, stirring constantly, until just bubbling. Remove from heat. Break egg white into a small bowl. Set aside. Beat the yolk into the hot pudding, blending well. Pour it into 2 to 3 custard cups. Heat oven to 450°F. (hot oven). Beat the egg white until stiff but not dry. Add the sugar, 1 tablespoon at a time, continuing to beat until the meringue is very stiff. Spoon a mound of it on top of each pudding; place them on a cookie sheet or in a shallow pan so that they won't tip between the wires of the oven rack. Brown in preheated oven for 2 minutes. Serve warm, topped with a blob of jelly. Makes 2 to 3.

Cheese Custard

1 cup milk
3 slices bread, crusts and all
1 tablespoon butter or margarine
3 slices packaged American cheese
2 eggs
½ teaspoon instant minced onion
⅛ teaspoon ground mustard
¼ teaspoon salt

Heat oven to 325°F. (moderately slow oven). In a saucepan slowly heat the milk until tiny bubbles form around the edge of the pan. Meanwhile grease a 1-quart casserole. Butter the bread and stack bread and cheese slices alternately in the greased baking dish, stacking them so that a cheese slice is on top. Beat eggs in a bowl and add onion, mustard and salt. Stir eggs into the milk and pour it into the baking dish, over and around the cheese. Set the casserole in a larger pan. Pour hot water around the casserole to within 1 inch of the top and bake in preheated oven for 1 hour. Makes 2 servings.

Oyster Milk Toast

¾ cup evaporated milk plus ½ cup water or
*   1¼ cups half milk half cream*
1 7-ounce can oysters, undrained
¼ teaspoon salt
Dash pepper
2 to 3 slices buttered toast or 4 pilot crackers

Heat milk and water or half and half in a saucepan until tiny bubbles begin to form around the edge of the pan. Add oysters, juice and all, salt and pepper. Heat slowly, until steaming hot. Serve over buttered toast or crackers. Makes 2 servings.

Shirred Eggs with Minced Ham

¼ cup light cream
¼ cup ground ham (ready-to-eat or leftover baked) or
    2 slices boiled ham, minced
2 eggs
Dash salt
Sprinkling of paprika

Heat oven to 375°F. (moderately hot oven). Grease 2 shirred-egg dishes or custard cups. Pour half of the cream into each. Sprinkle in the ham, dividing it equally between the two dishes. Break in the eggs. Sprinkle with salt and paprika. Bake in pre-heated oven for about 10 minutes, or until eggs are firm enough to suit you. Serve piping hot. Makes 2 servings.

Tomato Bouillon

Blend together in a small saucepan 1 6-ounce can V-8 cocktail, 1 chicken bouillon cube, and ½ cup water. Heat slowly. When bouillon cube is dissolved pour into 2 cups or mugs.

Baked Chicken with Spanish Rice

½ cup long-grain rice
1 12-ounce can V-8 juice
¼ teaspoon salt
Dash pepper
1 tablespoon minced onion
1 6-ounce can boneless chicken or
    1 cup coarsely diced cooked chicken
¼ cup grated American cheese

Heat oven to 375°F. (moderately hot oven). Combine rice, juice, salt, pepper, onion, and chicken in a greased 1-quart casserole. Cover and bake in preheated oven for 45 minutes. Remove cover and sprinkle rice mixture with the cheese. Continue to bake, uncovered, for 10 to 15 minutes, or until cheese is melted and rice dry and fluffy. Makes 2 generous servings.

Lemon Sponge Pudding

As nostalgic to many as Floating Island,* this was my first culinary accomplishment. First made by me at age twelve, it always softened Daddy's heart if a punishment was being considered. Too good to eat all at one sitting, this recipe makes 4 servings.

> ⅔ cup sugar
> 1½ tablespoons butter or margarine
> 2 teaspoons grated lemon rind
> 2 eggs
> 3 tablespoons flour
> ⅓ cup lemon juice
> 1 cup milk
> Dash salt

Heat oven to 350°F. (moderate oven). Cream together the sugar, butter, and lemon rind. Separate the eggs. Add the yolks to the sugar mixture and beat well. Stir in flour, lemon juice, and milk. Beat the egg whites and salt until stiff but not dry. Fold them into the yolk mixture. Pour into a greased 1-quart baking dish. Set it in a pan filled with 1 inch of hot water. Bake in preheated oven for 45 minutes. Makes 4 servings, equally good warm or chilled.

Spaghetti Creole

> *1½ cups cooked spaghetti (¾ cup uncooked)*
> *1 egg, well beaten*
> *1 8-ounce can tomato purée (or 1 cup)*
> *½ cup grated American cheese*
> *½ cup soft bread crumbs*
> *½ cup milk*
> *1 tablespoon diced onion*
> *½ teaspoon salt*
> *1 tablespoon chopped pimiento (optional)*
> *1 tablespoon parsley flakes*

Heat oven to 350°F. (moderate). Blend cooked spaghetti and the rest of the ingredients in a large bowl. Pour mixture into a well-greased 1-quart casserole and bake in preheated oven for 35 to 40 minutes or until steaming hot and cheese is melted. Makes 2 to 3 servings.

Salmon Loaf Supreme

> *1 6¾-ounce can salmon, undrained*
> *1 cup soft bread crumbs*
> *1 egg*
> *¼ cup milk*
> *1 teaspoon parsley flakes*
> *½ teaspoon instant minced onion*
> *½ teaspoon salt*
> *Dash pepper*
> *Lemon wedges*

Heat oven to 375°F. (moderately hot). Empty salmon, juice and all, into a bowl. Break it up with a fork. Add crumbs.

With a fork beat together the egg, milk, parsley flakes, onion, salt, and pepper. Stir into the salmon in the bowl. Grease a 6½″ × 4″ × 2½″ loaf pan or a small baking dish (one about 1-pint capacity). Spoon the salmon mixture into the pan. Bake in preheated oven for 30 minutes or until firm to the touch. Serve with lemon wedges. Makes 2 to 3 servings.

SLEEP TIGHT NIGHTCAPS

If appetites are less hearty than they should be during a soft-food regime, let a bedtime snack (best if it is a drinkable) give needed nourishment. For Sleep Tight Nightcaps that lull to sleep, serve a warm drink or one at room temperature. Serve it with a plain sugar cookie or cracker if you wish, not with rich cake or pastry—not at bedtime.

Prune Nog

⅔ cup bottled prune juice
1 teaspoon sugar
⅓ cup light cream
Sprinkling of cinnamon (optional)

Pour prune juice into a tall glass. Stir in sugar and cream. Sprinkle with cinnamon if desired. Makes 1 glass.

Banana Egg Nog

1 small ripe banana	1 cup milk
2 teaspoons sugar	1 egg
¼ teaspoon vanilla	Nutmeg

Peel and then mash the banana, using a fork. Add the sugar, vanilla, half of the milk, and the egg. Beat with an egg beater until blended. Stir in the rest of the milk. Pour into 2 glasses or cups. Sprinkle with nutmeg. Makes 2 servings.

Hot Spiced Grape Juice

1 cup bottled grape juice
¼ teaspoon grated lemon rind
4 whole cloves
Small stick cinnamon (about 1 inch long)
1 teaspoon sugar

Blend all ingredients in a small saucepan. Bring to a boil and simmer for 1 minute. Cool enough to drink with enjoyment. Pour into a mug or cup and serve. Makes 1 serving.

Hot Tea Punch

1 tea bag	2 teaspoons sugar
1 cup boiling water	Dash ground ginger
½ cup hot milk	

Place tea bag in a small saucepan and pour boiling water over it. Let steep for 3 minutes. Remove tea bag. Add remaining ingredients and serve. Makes 2 servings.

Chapter Five

MEALS FROM A
CAPSULE KITCHEN

Some of the Capsule Kitchen meals listed here, complete though they are, use only one automatic appliance. Other meals use two or three. Your entire kitchen, with the exception of the refrigerator, can be arranged on a serving cart or tea wagon. Sizes and prices of automatic fry pans, coffee makers, etc., vary, and no one but you can decide just which one is right for you.

Perhaps you will prefer a portable roaster-oven, large enough to roast a chicken and bake a cake both at the same time. Or you may choose a *tiny* table oven. One such little oven on the market today is about a foot square. Snoop, if you can, through the shops and take your time in determining which of the many appliances offered is right for your family of two. Don't have too many of them. Why set up an impressive array of shiny cooking units when you may need only two or three to serve your favorite meals?

Read carefully the directions which come with all electric cooking utensils. Always follow directions faithfully. They aren't hard to follow. And remember that all small automatic cooking utensils, even though they are not sitting over a flame on a range, get hot. They couldn't cook unless they did. So use pot holders. Even though the handles are of materials which can be touched when the pan is hot, don't risk rubbing a bare knuckle against a hot metal lid or surface.

Serve this complete meal with confidence if you have for a kitchen just an electric hot plate or automatic saucepan.

*Beef Stew with Noodles
Tossed Green Salad   French Dressing
Bread   Butter or Margarine
*Lemon Chiffon Pie for Two
Glass of Milk
Tea

Make the chiffon pie, if you choose, the night before, perhaps while preparing supper. With the pie chilling in the refrigerator, there is just the stew to cook. While eating dinner put the hot plate (or saucepan) back to work heating water for tea.

Beef Stew with Noodles

¾ pound beef chuck, cut in 1-inch pieces
1 tablespoon fat
2½ cups water
½ teaspoon Worcestershire sauce
1 small clove garlic, peeled
1 small onion, sliced
1 bay leaf
½ teaspoon salt
¼ teaspoon pepper
1½ cups packaged broad noodles
½ teaspoon caraway seeds (optional)

Brown meat on all sides in hot fat. Add water, Worcestershire sauce, garlic, onion, bay leaf, salt, and pepper. Cover pan and simmer for 1½ hours or until meat is very tender. Add a little more water from time to time, if necessary, to keep plenty of liquid boiling around the beef. Pour in the noodles and caraway seeds. Continue to cook for 10 minutes. Makes 2 generous servings.

Lemon Chiffon Pie for Two

1 tablespoon cold water
1 teaspoon unflavored gelatin
1 egg
4 tablespoons sugar
3 tablespoons lemon juice
Dash salt
½ teaspoon grated lemon rind
12 packaged vanilla wafers

Measure the cold water into a custard cup and sprinkle the gelatin over it. Let stand. Separate the egg. Combine the yolk, 2 tablespoons of the sugar, the lemon juice, salt, and lemon rind in the top of a double boiler. Beat with a spoon to blend. Set the top of the double boiler over boiling water and cook mixture, stirring constantly, until smooth and slightly thickened, about 5 minutes. Stir in the softened gelatin. Remove from heat. Beat egg white until stiff but not dry. Gradually beat in the remaining sugar, beating until meringue is stiff and glossy. Fold it into the hot lemon mixture. Line the bottom and sides of two 8-ounce glass baking dishes with the wafers. Pour lemon chiffon into the cookie crusts and chill. If made the same day, chill at least 1½ hours. Makes 2.

A tiny table oven (Redi-Baker) and a coffee maker prepare this pot roast dinner. There will be roast left for sandwiches another meal.

*Table Oven Pot Roast with Vegetables
Packaged Rolls   Butter or Margarine
Lettuce and Tomato Salad   Thousand Island Dressing
*Honey Graham Baked Bananas
Glass of Milk
Coffee

Table Oven Pot Roast with Vegetables

*1 pound round steak (a piece about 3 inches by
5 inches and 1¼ inch thick)*
2 medium-sized potatoes
2 medium-sized carrots
½ package dry onion soup

Plug in your table oven. Turn the dial to 425°F. (moderately hot). Place the round steak in the center of a piece of heavy-duty aluminum foil about 12 inches square. Peel the potatoes and scrape the carrots. Slice potatoes in ½-inch slices and the carrots even thinner. Arrange vegetables around the meat on the foil and pour the dry soup over. Wrap meat and vegetables in foil, folding the edges to seal in the juices. Place the foil packet in the oven tray. Close oven and bake at 425°F. for 1¼ hours or until vegetables are done. Seasoned to perfection with the soup, the meat has plenty of onion-flavored natural gravy. Makes 2 servings, plus meat for sandwiches another meal.

Honey Graham Baked Bananas

If you are using a tiny table oven, so small that it holds the pot roast and no more, these bananas will be ready when you are ready for them. They have plenty of time to bake while you eat your pot roast main course.

> *2 small firm bananas*
> *2 tablespoons honey*
> *1 tablespoon packaged graham cracker crumbs*
> *1 teaspoon butter or margarine*
> *Sprinkling of cinnamon*

Heat table oven to 425°F. (moderately hot). Peel bananas and place them on a square of aluminum foil. Crimp the edges of the foil around the sides of the bananas to hold in the juices. Drizzle bananas with honey. Sprinkle with cracker crumbs and dot with butter. Place foil "baking dish" with bananas in the oven. Close oven and bake for 8 to 10 minutes. Serve warm, sprinkled with cinnamon. Makes 2 servings.

An automatic sandwich grill or a portable roaster-oven will make this dinner preparation easy.

*Grilled Stuffed Hamburgers
*Broil-Browned Frozen Potato Patties
*Grilled Tomato Halves
Rolls or Bread   Butter or Margarine
Orange and Grapefruit Salad
French Dressing
*Freezer Tray Ice Cream Pudding
Glass of Milk
Tea or Coffee

Grilled Stuffed Hamburgers with Potato Patties and Tomato Halves

½ pound lean ground beef
1 slice packaged American cheese
Salt
Pepper
2 frozen potato patties, barely defrosted
1 firm tomato, cut in half crosswise

Divide the beef into 4 equal portions. Form each into a thin, round pattie. Cut the slice of cheese in half and fold each piece in two to form a small square of cheese. Place cheese squares in the center of two of the beef patties. Top with the two remaining patties and mold the edges together, sealing in the cheese. Sprinkle with salt and pepper.

If using a sandwich grill, heat at medium for 3 minutes. Open grids and grease them lightly. Arrange the hamburgers on one of the opened grids, the potato patties and tomato halves, cut sides down, on the other. Sprinkle potatoes and tomatoes with salt and pepper. Grill for 6 minutes. Turn beef, potato patties, and tomatoes. Grill for another 5 minutes. Sprinkle tomatoes with chives. Makes 2 servings.

If using a portable roaster-oven, bake meat patties at 450°F. (hot oven) for 12 to 15 minutes. Let the potato patties and tomato halves bake along with the hamburgers the last 10 minutes they bake.

Freezer Tray Ice Cream Pudding

½ pint vanilla ice cream
4 packaged fig bars, crumbled
½ teaspoon grated orange rind

Soften ice cream slightly. Pack half of it into an empty ice cube tray. Sprinkle it with the crumbled fig bars and the orange rind. Pack the rest of the ice cream over the crumb layer. Place in freezing compartment of refrigerator for at least one hour before serving. Makes 2 generous servings.

No need to apologize for this dinner. An automatic fry pan and a coffee maker make preparation easy.

*Asparagus Soup Shake
*Meat Balls with Spanish Rice
Peach and Cottage Cheese Salad
Packaged Corn Muffins   Butter or Margarine
*Chocolate Icebox Cake
Coffee

Asparagus Soup Shake

Let this soup shake double as a first course and a milk beverage.

> 1 10½-ounce can cream of asparagus soup
> 1 soup can of cold milk
> ½ teaspoon minced chives
> 2 wedges of lemon

In a pitcher or plastic shaker mix the soup and milk to a froth. Pour it into two tall tumblers. Sprinkle with chives and serve with a wedge of lemon.

Meat Balls with Spanish Rice

> ¼ *pound ground lean beef*
> ½ *teaspoon salt*
> *Dash pepper*
> *1 slice bread*
> *1 egg, beaten*
> *1 tablespoon catsup*
> *2 tablespoons salad oil or shortening*
> *1 small green pepper, minced*
> *1 small onion, thinly sliced*
> ½ *cup raw rice*
> ¾ *cup tomato juice*
> ¾ *cup water*
> ½ *teaspoon salt*
> *1 teaspoon chili powder* (*optional*)

Combine beef, ½ teaspoon salt, and pepper in a bowl. Tear bread into crumbs. Add crumbs, egg, and catsup to meat. Blend well. Form into 6 small balls. Start heating fry pan to 350°F. Heat salad oil in pan and brown meat balls, turning to brown all sides. Add green pepper and onion. Turn heat to 250°F. (simmer). Cook vegetables for 2 minutes. Then add rice, tomato juice, water, salt, and chili powder. Stir and cover pan. Cook for 25 to 35 minutes or until rice is tender and moisture absorbed. Makes 2 generous servings.

Chocolate Icebox Cake

> ½ *cup heavy cream*   ¼ *teaspoon vanilla extract*
> *10 packaged chocolate icebox wafers*

Whip cream stiff. Stir in vanilla. Spread each wafer with whipped cream. Stack spread wafers. Turn the stack on its side on a serving plate and press it together to form a cylinder of cookies with cream between. Spread the top and sides with the rest of the whipped cream. Chill at least 3 hours or overnight. Slice in diagonal slices. Makes 2 to 3 servings.

A toaster and hot plate or electric saucepan prepare this dinner in a jiffy.

Small Glass of Grape Juice
*Tuna and Vegetable Rabbit on Toast
Vegetable Slaw   Sour Cream Dressing*
Bread or Rolls   Butter or Margarine
Frozen Ice Cream Cake Roll (from your supermarket)
Glass of Milk or Tea

Tuna and Vegetable Rabbit on Toast

1 tablespoon butter or margarine
1 tablespoon flour
1 cup milk or ½ cup each evaporated milk and water
½ cup grated Cheddar cheese
¼ teaspoon salt
¼ teaspoon dry mustard
1 3½-ounce can tuna
½ cup canned peas or cooked mixed vegetables, drained
2 to 3 slices buttered toast

Melt butter in saucepan. Add flour and blend. Stir in milk and cook over low heat (or with saucepan set to simmer), stirring constantly until thick. Add cheese and seasonings. Stir until cheese is melted (about 1 minute). Stir in tuna and peas or vegetables. Serve over hot buttered toast. Makes 2 generous servings.

Chapter Six

FOR SPECIAL OCCASIONS

Are the children and grandchildren coming to dinner? Is your church sewing circle or lodge having a potluck? What to serve? What to take that isn't too expensive and too nerve-racking to prepare? If your home is to be the scene of the festivities, keep the menu simple. Plan one that can be prepared, for the most part, in a leisurely fashion the day ahead. Then you, too, can relax and enjoy your party.

If it is a potluck and your contribution is to be a baked dish, a salad, or dessert to serve 6 or 8, plan one requiring little last-minute fuss and bother. With these few menus and recipes for dinners at home, you can make yourself a reputation as the best cook in the family. When they have tasted one of your potluck specials, they'll soon learn to save room for whatever dish *you* take.

MENU FOR A HOLIDAY DINNER AT HOME

*Small Roast Turkey with Dressing   Gravy
Baked Sweet Potatoes and/or Instant Mashed Potatoes
Buttered Frozen Peas with Canned Sliced Mushrooms
Cranberry Sauce   Celery   Olives
Rolls   Butter or Margarine
Canned Plum Pudding with *Hard Sauce
or
*Festive Pumpkin Ice Cream Pie
Tea or Coffee   Milk

Small Roast Turkey with Dressing

News today is the small 4- to 8-pound, ready-to-cook-weight turkey, called often a fryer-roaster turkey. Available fresh or frozen, these small birds are tender and juicy with less bone per pound than their ancestors of ten years ago. For five or six people choose one about 5 or 6 pounds. If you love leftover turkey, choose one a bit larger. Even a 7-pound turkey, stuffed and ready to roast, is fairly light to handle.

Almost everyone today knows that it is not safe to stuff a turkey the day ahead. That is one of the day-ahead procedures we have had to give up. Dangerous bacteria, sometimes fatal, can grow overnight. Clean your turkey the day ahead, even make the stuffing (if convenient) the night before, but chill it thoroughly in a shallow pan, *not in* the turkey. The dressing in the center of a turkey stuffed a day ahead of roasting might not be chilled in time to make it safe to eat.

Stuff your turkey just before you are ready to roast it with either of these two stuffings, one sage-seasoned or one fruit-flavored. Roast it in an oven preheated to 325°F. (slow to moderate oven) for 30 minutes per pound, or about 3 hours for a 6-pound bird.

Savory Sage Dressing

10 slices enriched white bread or
  1 8-ounce package stuffing mix
½ cup butter, margarine, or bacon drippings
½ cup minced onion
½ cup chopped celery
1 teaspoon salt
⅛ teaspoon pepper
2 teaspoons crushed sage

Remove the crusts from the bread. Cut it into tiny cubes. Dry the cubes about 20 minutes in a very slow oven (250°F.). Or use packaged stuffing mix. Heat together in a skillet the butter, margarine, or bacon drippings, onion, celery, salt, pepper, and sage. Cover the pan and simmer for 10 minutes. Add the butter mixture to bread cubes or stuffing mix. Toss with a fork to mix thoroughly.

This makes a dry, fluffy dressing. If you prefer one more moist, add ½ cup water to the vegetables while they cook. Makes enough to stuff a 6-pound turkey.

Dried-Fruit Dressing

10 slices enriched white bread or
  1 8-ounce package stuffing mix
¼ cup butter or margarine
¼ cup chopped celery
1 teaspoon salt
½ cup seedless raisins
½ cup cut-up dried apricots

Make bread into cubes as in the Savory Sage Dressing* or use the packaged mix. Then heat together in a skillet the

butter or margarine, celery, salt, raisins, and apricots. Cover
and simmer for 10 minutes. Add the butter and fruit mixture
to the bread cubes or stuffing mix and toss to blend. Makes
enough to stuff a 6-pound turkey.

Festive Pumpkin Ice Cream Pie

Made in about one fourth the time that it takes to bake a
traditional pumpkin pie, this wonderful newcomer to the
pumpkin pie family almost makes itself.

> *½ package piecrust mix (about 1 cup or 1 stick)*
> *3 tablespoons soft butter or margarine*
> *2 tablespoons cold water*
> *1 pint vanilla ice cream*
> *1½ cups canned pumpkin*
> *¼ teaspoon ground allspice*
> *¼ teaspoon ground cloves*
> *½ teaspoon ground cinnamon*
> *¼ teaspoon salt*
> *⅓ cup milk*
> *1 package instant vanilla pudding mix*

For a crust so flaky that everyone will swear you made it
from your secret recipe, blend together the piecrust mix, soft
butter, and water, tossing lightly with a fork. Press dough
into a ball and roll it out on a well-floured pastry cloth or
board. Fit the crust into an 8-inch pie pan. Flute the edges
and prick the entire surface of the crust with a fork to prevent it from shrinking while baking. Bake at 425°F. (moderately hot oven) for 10 to 12 minutes, or until nicely browned.
Cool ½ hour. Then empty the ice cream into a bowl and
let it soften. Combine the pumpkin, spices, and salt in another
bowl. Add the milk and pudding mix. Beat with an egg

beater for 1 minute. Add softened ice cream and beat just to blend. Pour into the cool pie shell and chill at least 3 hours or overnight. Makes one 8-inch pie or enough for six.

Hard Sauce

> ⅓ cup butter or margarine
> 1 cup sifted confectioners' sugar
> 1 teaspoon vanilla or rum flavoring
> ½ teaspoon grated lemon rind (optional)
> Pinch salt

Work the butter with the back of a spoon until light and creamy. Add sugar gradually, beating until light and fluffy. Add the extract, a few drops at a time, then the lemon rind and salt. Makes 6 servings.

MENU FOR A FAMILY GET-TOGETHER

Roast Half Leg of Lamb with Mint Jelly Glaze
or
No-Carve Stuffed Pork Roast
with Spiced Crab Apples
Tiny Roasted Potatoes and Onions
Buttered Frozen Green Beans
Finely Grated Cabbage and Carrot Slaw   *Old-Fashioned
Boiled Dressing
Rolls   Butter or Margarine
*Jelly Ice Cream Roll
or
*Fudge Frosted Layer Cake
Coffee or Tea   Milk

Old-Fashioned Boiled Dressing

2 teaspoons dry mustard
3 tablespoons sugar
½ teaspoon salt
Speck cayenne pepper
2 tablespoons flour
⅓ cup cider vinegar
½ cup water
4 egg yolks or 2 eggs, well beaten
1 tablespoon butter or margarine
Light cream or evaporated milk

In the top of a double boiler, over simmering water, combine mustard, sugar, salt, pepper, and flour. Stir in the vinegar and water. Blend well. Cook, stirring constantly, until the mixture is smooth and thickened, about 4 minutes. Pour half of the hot mixture into the beaten egg yolks or eggs, stirring to blend. Stir this back into the hot mixture left in the double boiler. Cook, stirring until thick enough to mound. Remove from heat and stir in the butter or margarine. Cover and cool. Store in the refrigerator. Thin, when using, with a little light cream or evaporated milk. Makes about 1¼ cups dressing.

Jelly Ice Cream Roll

1 pint vanilla ice cream
1 packaged jelly roll cake
2 tablespoons confectioners' sugar

Let ice cream soften enough that it spreads easily but is not runny. Unroll jelly roll and spread with ice cream. Roll up again and wrap in transparent Saran-Wrap or aluminum foil. Freeze until serving time. Then sprinkle the cake with the confectioners' sugar and slice. Makes 5 to 6 servings.

Fudge Frosted Layer Cake

A one-egg cake made for pennies a serving, this one boasts a fudge frosting that never gets grainy and requires no beating.

> 1¾ cups sifted cake flour
> 1 cup sugar
> 2½ teaspoons baking powder
> ½ teaspoon salt
> ¼ cup shortening
> 1 egg
> ¾ cup milk
> 1 teaspoon vanilla extract

Heat oven to 375°F. (moderately hot). Grease two 8-inch round cake pans well. Dust them with flour. Sift together the 1¾ cups sifted cake flour, sugar, baking powder, and salt. Stir the shortening just enough to soften it and add it to the flour mixture. Add the unbeaten egg, half of the milk. Beat 2 minutes by hand or 1½ minutes on electric mixer at medium speed. Add the rest of the milk and the vanilla. Continue to beat another 2 minutes by hand or 1½ minutes by mixer. Pour batter into prepared pans and bake for 25 minutes in preheated oven, or until done. If cake springs back without leaving an imprint when lightly touched on the top, it's done. Cool 10 minutes on wire cake racks. Remove from pans. Fill and frost with Creamy Fudge Frosting.*

Creamy Fudge Frosting

> ¾ cup evaporated milk
> 1⅔ cups sugar
> ¼ teaspoon salt
> 1½ cups miniature marshmallows or diced large marsh-
>   mallows
> 1½ cups semisweet chocolate bits
> 1 teaspoon vanilla

Combine milk and sugar in a 2-quart aluminum saucepan (the fudge is more apt to scorch in glass). Stir over medium heat until sugar is dissolved and the mixture begins to boil vigorously. Turn heat low and continue to cook, stirring constantly for 4 minutes. Remove from heat. Stir in the marshmallows and chocolate, stirring 1 to 2 minutes or until marshmallows are dissolved. Add vanilla. Cool and use to frost cake.

Or, for the creamiest fudge you ever ate, a fudge that never gets grainy and doesn't need a candy thermometer, use ⅔ cup evaporated milk instead of ¾ cup. Cook the mixture for 5 minutes instead of 4. Stir in the marshmallows, chocolate and vanilla as for the fudge frosting. Pour fudge into a greased 8-inch square pan. Cool slightly and cut into squares.

No-Carve Stuffed Pork Roast with Spiced Crab Apples

> 1 pork loin roast, 6 ribs long (4 to 4½ pounds)
> 1 package prepared stuffing mix
> ¼ cup butter or margarine
> ¼ cup chopped onion
> ½ cup chopped green pepper
> ½ teaspoon salt
> ⅓ cup water

Have the butcher cut the roast into 6 separate chops. Empty stuffing into a bowl. Heat the butter in a saucepan; add onion, green pepper, and salt. Cook slowly for 3 minutes. Add the water. Bring to a boil and stir the onion mixture into the stuffing mix, tossing to blend. Place a mound of stuffing on each of 5 chops. Press all 6 chops back together, forming a dressing-stuffed roast. Push a long skewer through to hold firmly in place. Roast, uncovered, at 325°F. (slow to moderate oven) for 1½ to 2 hours. Arrange on a serving platter. Garnish with crab apples. Remove skewer and serve. Makes 5 servings with 1 extra chop for the biggest eater.

MENU FOR A BACK-YARD OR PORCH PARTY

Assorted Cold Cuts
*Mealy Potato Salad
Marinated Sliced Tomatoes and Asparagus Tips
Buttered Rolls (buttered in advance)
*Jellied Grape and Melon Ring with Cinnamon Sour Cream
Packaged Cookies
Tea   Hot or Cold

Mealy Potato Salad

6 medium-sized potatoes
1 tablespoon grated onion
1 teaspoon salt
¼ teaspoon pepper
4 hard-cooked eggs
½ cup mayonnaise
1 teaspoon prepared mustard
Crisp lettuce leaves

Wash potatoes and cook them in their jackets in boiling water until very tender. Cool them enough to handle easily, then skin, dice, and mash slightly with a fork. Add onion, salt, and pepper. Dice eggs and add. In a cup blend the mayonnaise and mustard. Fold dressing into warm salad. Chill to blend the flavors—at least 2 hours. Serve garnished with crisp lettuce. Makes 6 servings.

Jellied Grape and Melon Ring with Cinnamon Sour Cream

> 2 packages grape Jello
> 3½ cups water
> 2½ cups melon balls
> 1 8-ounce carton commercial sour cream
> 1 tablespoon sugar
> ½ teaspoon ground cinnamon

Make the Jello the day ahead. Follow package directions, but use the 3½ cups water instead of 4 cups called for when preparing 2 packages. When mixture is cool, thick, and syrupy, add the melon balls. Pour into a 5- or 6-cup ring mold. Chill overnight. Stir the sugar and cinnamon into the sour cream. Chill.

To serve: Dip the ring mold into hot water and unmold it onto a chilled serving plate. Pile cinnamon sour cream into the center of the jellied ring. Makes 6 to 8 servings.

POTLUCK SPECIALS TO SERVE SIX OR EIGHT

If the committee asks you to bring a hot dish, these are made to order. You'll hardly need to wash up the dish! Not that the recipes don't make enough to serve 6 or 8 . . . but the platter will be scraped clean.

Baked Macaroni and Ham Loaf

Serve with Horse-Radish Sauce.*

>   *¾ cup elbow macaroni*
>   *1½ cups milk*
>   *2 tablespoons butter or margarine*
>   *1 cup soft bread crumbs*
>   *1 chopped pimiento*
>   *1 tablespoon parsley flakes*
>   *1 tablespoon instant minced onion*
>   *1½ cups packaged grated American cheese*
>   *½ teaspoon salt*
>   *⅛ teaspoon pepper*
>   *3 eggs, well beaten*
>   *1½ cups ground ready-to-eat ham*

Cook macaroni as package directs. Drain well. Heat milk with butter. When small bubbles form around the edge of the milk, pour it over the bread crumbs in a mixing bowl. Add pimiento, parsley, onion, cheese, salt, and pepper. Slowly stir in the beaten eggs, then the ham. Pour the mixture into a greased 9″ × 5″ × 3″ loaf pan. If you are starting this loaf the day ahead of the potluck or picnic, place it in the refrigerator now and let it stay there until 1½ hours before you need to start with it in hand.

Then take it out of the refrigerator and let it warm to room temperature while preheating the oven to 325°F. (slow to moderate oven). Bake the loaf for 1 hour. Cool for 5 minutes. Then wrap securely in aluminum foil. Wrap again in three thicknesses of heavy brown paper or newspaper. And off you go. Unmold it at the church or picnic grounds and enjoy it—still hot enough to call hot. Makes 6 to 8 servings. Serve, if desired, with Horse-Radish Sauce.*

Horse-Radish Sauce

> ½ cup mayonnaise or Old-Fashioned Boiled Dressing*
> ¼ cup chili sauce
> 1 teaspoon Worcestershire sauce
> 3 tablespoons bottled horse-radish

Mix all ingredients. Pour into a 1-cup jar, cover, and chill. Makes about 1 cup.

Mary's Potluck Casserole

Why "Mary's Casserole"? Well, Mary, who is just like one of our family, gave it to us. It's always been "Mary's Casserole."

> ½ pound bulk sausage
> 1 onion, minced
> 1 6-ounce can sliced mushrooms, undrained
> 1 6-ounce package sliced almonds
> 1 cup uncooked rice
> 1 package dry chicken noodle soup
> ½ teaspoon salt
> 3 cups water

Fry sausage meat over low heat, stirring it frequently to break it into bits. When lightly browned add the onion and cook a few minutes until onion is tender but not brown. Drain off fat. Mix sausage and onion with the remaining ingredients. Pour mixture into a greased 2-quart baking dish. This much can be done a day ahead of time. Cover casserole and chill until 1½ hours before going to the supper get-together. Then remove casserole from the refrigerator to warm to room temperature while preheating oven to 350°F. (moderate oven). Bake covered, for 40 minutes, then uncover for 15 minutes or until all moisture is absorbed. Makes 6 to 8 servings. To keep warm until suppertime wrap it first in foil, then in several thicknesses of heavy brown paper or newspaper.

If your pot-luck contribution is to be a salad, either of these will be welcome. You had better write off copies of the recipes in advance. You are sure to have requests.

Rice and Shrimp Salad

> *1 pound cooked fresh shrimp or*
> > *2 cans (4½ ounces drained weight each)*
> *1 cup cooked, chilled rice*
> *2 to 3 scallions*
> *¼ cup chopped, stuffed olives*
> *¼ cup minced green pepper*
> *¼ cup thinly sliced radishes (optional)*
> *1 tablespoon lemon juice*
> *¾ teaspoon salt*
> *2 tablespoons French dressing*
> *⅓ cup mayonnaise*
> *Crisp lettuce leaves*

If using fresh shrimp, buy them cooked. Or cook them the day ahead of time and chill. Cook rice. Slice scallions, tops and all. Chop olives and mince green pepper. Slice radishes, too, if you like their bity flavor. Put shrimp, rice, and vegetables in a bowl. Cover and chill until you are almost ready to leave for your potluck. Then add lemon juice, salt, French dressing, and mayonnaise, tossing lightly to blend. Line a salad bowl with lettuce leaves and pile the salad into it. Wrap in foil, then several thicknesses of newspaper to keep the salad chilled. Makes 6 servings.

Pineapple Hash Salad

> 1 1-pound can crushed pineapple
> 4 cups shredded cabbage, packed
> 1½ cups miniature marshmallows
> ½ teaspoon salt
> ¼ teaspoon dry mustard
> ½ cup mayonnaise
> ⅛ teaspoon anise seed (optional)

In the morning or the day ahead, drain the pineapple. Grate the cabbage on a coarse grater. Chill pineapple and cabbage until half an hour or so before you want to be ready to leave the house. Then, in a large bowl, combine cabbage, drained pineapple, marshmallows, and salt. In a cup blend the mustard, mayonnaise, and anise seed. (Use the anise if you and your cronies like a hint of licorice flavor.) Toss with a fork to blend well. Makes 6 to 8 servings.

For easy carrying put the salad in a plastic bowl or shaker with a cover. It can't break, and it makes a light package to carry.

Make these two desserts, best when slightly warm, early on the day of the party. Wrap them, while still hot, in foil, then three layers of newspaper. Standing at room temperature, they will stay warm.

Deep Dish Apple Pie with Cheese Crumb Topping

> *6 cups thinly sliced tart apples (7 to 8 apples)*
> *¾ cup sugar*
> *2 tablespoons flour*
> *¼ teaspoon salt*
> *1 teaspoon cinnamon*
> *¼ teaspoon nutmeg*
> *1 teaspoon lemon rind*
> *2 tablespoons lemon juice*
> *1 cup (half package) piecrust mix*
> *⅔ cup packaged grated American cheese*
> *3 tablespoons brown sugar*
> *2 tablespoons soft butter or margarine*

Early in the day heat the oven to 400°F. (moderately hot). Measure sliced apples into a bowl. Mix sugar, flour, salt, cinnamon, nutmeg, lemon rind, and juice. Pour sugar mixture over apples and toss with a fork to coat them. Pour apples into a greased 1½-quart baking dish and bake in preheated oven for 40 minutes. Meanwhile combine piecrust mix, cheese, brown sugar, and butter or margarine in a bowl. Toss lightly with a fork to blend.

At the end of the 40 minutes sprinkle cheese mixture over the apples and continue to bake for 15 to 20 more minutes or until apples are tender and crumbs lightly browned. Makes 6 to 8 servings. Serve warm, with or without cream.

Peach and Gingerbread Upside Down Cake

3 tablespoons butter or margarine
1 1-pound can peach halves
1 package gingerbread mix
⅓ cup brown sugar, packed
Maraschino cherries or seedless raisins

Heat oven to 350°F. (moderate oven). Measure the butter or margarine into a 9-inch square cake pan and set it in the oven to melt while you are opening the can of peaches and the package of gingerbread mix. Remove the pan of melted butter from the oven and sprinkle in the brown sugar. Drain the peach halves and arrange them, cut side down, over the sugar-butter mixture in the pan. Prepare gingerbread mix as package directs and carefully pour it over the peach layer. Bake in preheated oven for 30 minutes. Cool in pan for 10 minutes on a wire cake rack. Then invert cake onto a serving plate and insert a cherry or raisins where the pit was removed from the peaches. Serve warm, with or without cream. Makes 6 to 8 servings.

Chapter Seven

FOR THOSE WHO
LIVE ALONE

If you are one of the retired people living alone, don't feel alone. There are many like you. Pamper yourself with such good meals, served so handsomely, that even though eaten alone, they are meals to look forward to. Make sure you don't slip into habits of refrigerator nibbling just because there is no one but yourself to impress with your cooking.

The chances are that at least once a week you will be invited out to dinner. Once a week, perhaps, you will attend a club or church dinner. Then once or twice a week, no doubt, you will entertain a friend. That leaves three or four dinner meals to prepare and serve in style to yourself.

Breakfasts and suppers aren't a problem when cooking for one. Eggs, fruits, juices, cereals, sandwiches, soups—all make these meals simple to prepare for a family of one. Dinners will be easier to shop for and less expensive if you plan three meals from the same cut of meat. Once the main meat dish is settled, small cans of vegetables or part of a package of frozen vegetables, ice cream, canned or fresh fruits, individually packaged cake slices or cupcakes give ready variety without waste from leftovers.

To help plan that problem child, the main dish to serve one person, here are twelve menus, each different. Three are planned using one small chicken, three use a total of one pound of ground lean beef, three a pound of round steak and a 5-rib pork roast supplies the meat for the last three main dishes.

One 2½-pound broiler-fryer cut in serving pieces gives you your meat for these three different dinners.

*Chicken with Orange Sauce
Quick-Cooking Rice
Buttered Broccoli
Tomato Salad
Roll or Melba Toast   Butter or Margarine
Canned Kadota Figs with Cream
Half Glass of Milk
Tea or Coffee

Small Glass of Grapefruit Juice
*Chicken Divan
Tossed Salad
Packaged Corn Muffin   Butter or Margarine
Baked Apple or Ice Cream
Half Glass of Milk
Tea or Coffee

*Chicken Tetrazzini
Buttered Peas
Fruit Salad
Melba Toast or Crackers
Packaged Marble Cake Slice à la Mode
Coffee or Tea

Chicken with Orange Sauce

1 breast piece of chicken or 1 drumstick and 1 thigh
1 tablespoon flour
¼ teaspoon salt
Dash pepper
2 teaspoons shortening
2 tablespoons frozen orange juice concentrate
½ cup water
Dash of nutmeg

Wash chicken and dry it well with a paper towel. Combine flour, salt, and pepper in a pie pan. Roll chicken in flour mixture, coating it well. Heat shortening in a small skillet. Brown chicken in hot fat over low heat, turning to brown all sides. Add the orange juice concentrate and water (or use ⅔ cup fresh or canned orange juice). Cover and cook over very low heat for 25 to 30 minutes or until chicken is tender. "Peek" occasionally and add a bit more water, if necessary, to keep juice simmering around chicken. Add a dash of nutmeg and serve with fluffy quick-cooking rice. Makes 1 serving.

Boil the remaining chicken (all but the pieces used for the Chicken with Orange Sauce.* When tender, divide it in half. Use half for Chicken Divan* and keep the rest in the refrigerator for Chicken Tetrazzini.*

Chicken Divan

½ package frozen broccoli
Cooked chicken (half left from Chicken with Orange
    Sauce)*
½ cup cream of chicken soup
1 tablespoon grated Parmesan cheese

Heat oven to 350°F. (moderate). Cook broccoli in boiling salted water as package directs. Drain. Pick chicken from bones, leaving it in large pieces. Grease an 8-inch pie pan. Arrange broccoli over the bottom of the pan. Top it with chicken and pour the soup over. Sprinkle with the cheese and bake in preheated oven for 30 minutes or until lightly browned and bubbling hot. Makes 1 serving.

Chicken Tetrazzini

> ½ cup spaghetti broken in 2-inch lengths
> Cooked chicken (half left from Chicken with Orange
>   Sauce*)
> ½ cup cream of chicken soup
> ¼ cup milk
> ½ teaspoon instant minced onion
> ⅓ cup grated Cheddar cheese
> 1 teaspoon parsley flakes
> ½ teaspoon Worcestershire sauce (optional)

Cook spaghetti in 3 cups of boiling water. Drain. Dice chicken. Combine cooked spaghetti, chicken, and remaining ingredients in the top of a double boiler. Set boiler top in place over boiling water and cook for 20 minutes, or until cheese is melted and mixture steaming hot. Makes 1 serving.

With one pound of lean ground beef you have the meat for these three different dinners.

Broiled Ground Beef Pattie (one third of the beef)
Browned Frozen Potato Pattie
Buttered Green Beans

Lettuce Salad   Thousand Island Dressing
Roll or Melba Toast   Butter or Margarine
*Honey-Glazed Canned Pear Half
Half Glass of Milk
Tea or Coffee

*Individual Meat Loaf
Baked Potato
Buttered Broccoli or other Green Vegetable
Pear and Cottage Cheese Salad
Assorted Crackers or Melba Toast
*Fruit Whip
Half Glass of Milk
Tea or Coffee

Spaghetti with *Meat Sauce   Grated Parmesan Cheese
Tossed Salad
Bread Sticks or Melba Toast
Ice Cream   Packaged Cupcake
Tea or Coffee

Honey-Glazed Pear Half

1 canned pear half
1 tablespoon honey
Dash cinnamon

Heat broiler. Place pear half, rounded side down, on a piece of aluminum foil about 6 inches square. Crimp the edges of the foil up around the sides of the pear. Spoon the honey over the pear and sprinkle it with cinnamon. Broil 5 inches from heat for 2 to 3 minutes. Serve warm. Makes 1 serving.

Individual Meat Loaf

⅓ pound ground beef
½ teaspoon instant minced onion
¼ teaspoon salt
1 tablespoon chili sauce
1 egg yolk, slightly beaten
1 tablespoon milk
2 tablespoons cracker crumbs

Heat oven to 375°F. (moderately hot oven). Combine all ingredients in a small bowl. Blend well. Pack mixture into a greased custard cup and bake in preheated oven for 25 minutes. Makes 1 serving.

Fruit Whip

Here is the way to use that leftover egg white—left from the Individual Meat Loaf.*

1 canned peach half or 4 stewed prunes
1 egg white
2 tablespoons sugar
⅛ teaspoon cinnamon
¼ teaspoon grated lemon rind (optional)

Mash peach half or pit prunes and cut them into bits. Beat the egg white stiff. Gradually beat in the sugar, continuing to beat until egg white stands in stiff peaks when beater is raised. Fold in the fruit, cinnamon, and rind. Makes 1 serving.

Meat Sauce

2 teaspoons olive or salad oil
⅓ pound ground beef
1 small onion, minced, or 2 teaspoons instant minced
 onion
1 8-ounce can spaghetti sauce with mushrooms
¼ teaspoon salt
⅛ teaspoon pepper
Cooked spaghetti
Grated Parmesan cheese

Heat oil in a small skillet. Break the beef into bits and brown it in the hot oil. Add onion and cook 1 minute. Add spaghetti sauce, salt, pepper. Simmer for 10 minutes. Meanwhile cook about 1/6 of a pound of spaghetti in boiling, salted water as package directs. Drain well. Serve sauce over spaghetti. Sprinkle with the Parmesan cheese. Makes 1 very generous serving, so generous that your salad and dessert can afford to be a bit skimpy this time.

Buy one pound of round steak cut 1 inch thick. Divide it in thirds—one third to use when preparing each of these menus.

*Swiss Steak
Parsley Buttered Potato
Canned or Frozen Wax Beans
Tossed Green Salad
Slices of Canned Date Nut Bread   Cream Cheese and Jelly
Half Glass of Milk
Tea or Coffee

*Beef Stew with Noodles
Buttered Carrots
Lettuce and Tomato Salad
Roll or Melba Toast   Butter or Margarine
Frozen Melon Balls in Grape Juice
Half Glass of Milk
Tea or Coffee

Hot Tomato Juice
*Individual Beef and Vegetable Pie
with Mashed Potato Border
Crisp Green Salad
Melba Toast or Buttered Roll
Applesauce   Gingersnaps
Glass of Milk

Swiss Steak

⅓ pound round steak cut 1 inch thick
2 teaspoons flour
¼ teaspoon salt
Dash pepper
2 teaspoons salad oil or shortening
1 cup tomato juice
1 medium onion, peeled and sliced

Lay meat on a breadboard. Sprinkle it with half of the flour
and the salt and pepper. Pound in the flour using the rim of a
sturdy saucer or a meat pounder. Turn meat and pound in
the rest of the flour into the other side. Heat the oil or shortening in a skillet with a cover. Brown meat well on both sides
over medium heat. Add tomato juice and onion slices. Cover
and simmer for 1 hour, adding a little water from time to time
if necessary, to keep meat from sticking. Makes 1 serving.

Beef Stew with Noodles

⅓ pound round steak
2 teaspoons flour
¼ teaspoon salt
Dash pepper
2 teaspoons salad oil
Bay leaf
1 teaspoon instant minced onion
1½ cups water
1 cup packaged noodles

Cut beef into 1-inch cubes. Combine flour, salt, and pepper. Roll beef in flour mixture, coating well. Heat oil in a heavy saucepan with cover. Brown beef well on all sides in oil. Add the bay leaf, onion, and water. Cover and simmer for 1 hour or until meat is very tender. Sprinkle in the noodles, adding a little more water, if necessary, to keep liquid boiling around the noodles. Cover and cook for 10 minutes. Makes 1 hearty serving.

Individual Beef and Vegetable Pie with Mashed Potato Border

⅓ pound round steak
2 teaspoons flour
¼ teaspoon salt
Dash pepper
2 teaspoons salad oil
1½ cups water
1 medium onion
1 carrot
¾ cup instant whipped potato flakes
½ cup water
1 teaspoon butter or margarine
Salt

Cut beef in 1-inch cubes. Combine flour, salt, and pepper. Roll beef in flour mixture, coating well. Heat oil in a heavy saucepan with cover. Brown meat in oil, turning to brown all sides. Add the 1½ cups water. Bring to a boil. Cover pan and simmer for 45 minutes. Meanwhile peel onion and slice it. Scrape carrot and cut it in half. Add the vegetables to the beef and cook until tender, about 20 minutes, adding a bit more water to the pan, if necessary, to keep beef and vegetables from sticking. Measure the potato flakes, the ½ cup water, and butter or margarine. Prepare whipped potatoes as package directs. Add a dash of salt. Serve beef and vegetables in a ramekin bordered with whipped potatoes. Makes 1 serving.

One 5-rib pork roast—three main dishes for these tasty meals. Have your butcher cut off two ribs as one thick chop. Then have him cut a pocket in the chop for stuffing (for Baked Stuffed Pork Chop*). Roast the 3 ribs. Serve once as roast pork and use the leftover roast to make Sweet and Sour Pork* another meal.

Roast Pork   Cream Gravy
Pickled Crab Apples or Canned Applesauce
Baked Sweet Potato
Buttered Spinach with Lemon
Buttered Roll or Melba Toast
Mixed Fruit Compote
Packaged Cookies
Half Glass of Milk
Your Choice of Beverage

*Sweet and Sour Pork
Steamed Rice
Lettuce Salad   Russian Dressing
Buttered Roll or Bread
Packaged Almond Cookies
Half Glass of Milk
Tea

Sweet and Sour Pork

Leftover pork roast
1 teaspoon shortening
1 slice canned pineapple or ¼ cup drained canned pine-
   apple chunks
½ cup pineapple juice
1 small onion, thinly sliced or 1 scallion, cut in 1-inch
   lengths
¼ teaspoon salt
1 teaspoon vinegar
1 tablespoon brown sugar
⅛ teaspoon ground ginger
1 teaspoon soy sauce
½ teaspoon cornstarch

Dice pork. Brown it in a small saucepan in hot shortening. Cut the pineapple into 6 or 8 pieces (or use canned tidbits). Add pineapple, pineapple juice, onion slices, salt, and vinegar. Cover pan and simmer for 5 minutes. Meanwhile blend together the remaining ingredients. Stir the cornstarch mixture into the pork, stirring constantly until sauce is clear and slightly thickened. Serve over rice. Makes 1 serving.

Baked Stuffed Pork Chop

1 double pork chop
Salt
¼ cup coarsely crumbled saltine cracker crumbs
½ teaspoon parsley flakes
¼ teaspoon instant minced onion
1 3-ounce can sliced mushrooms

Heat oven to 350°F. (moderate). Sprinkle the inside of the pocket in the chop with salt. Combine the cracker crumbs, parsley flakes, and onion. Drain mushrooms, saving juice. Add the mushrooms to the crumb mixture and toss with a fork to blend the stuffing. Spoon stuffing into the pocket in the chop. Place stuffed chop in a 1-quart casserole or a small baking dish with a cover. Pour the drained mushroom liquid around the chop. Cover and bake in preheated oven for 1 hour. Uncover and continue to bake for 10 to 15 minutes, or until chop is well browned and tender. Makes 1 serving.

Index

44318